CONSTELLATIONS

Like the future itself, the imaginative possibilities of science fiction are limitless. And the very development of cinema is inextricably linked to the genre, which, from the earliest depictions of space travel and the robots of silent cinema to the immersive 3D wonders of contemporary blockbusters, has continually pushed at the boundaries. **Constellations** provides a unique opportunity for writers to share their passion for science fiction cinema in a book-length format, each title devoted to a significant film from the genre. Writers place their chosen film in a variety of contexts – generic, institutional, social, historical – enabling **Constellations** to map the terrain of science fiction cinema from the past to the present... and the future.

'This stunning, sharp series of books fills a real need for authoritative, compact studies of key science fiction films. Written in a direct and accessible style by some of the top critics in the field, brilliantly designed, lavishly illustrated and set in a very modern typeface that really shows off the text to best advantage, the volumes in the **Constellations** series promise to set the standard for SF film studies in the 21st century.'
Wheeler Winston Dixon, Ryan Professor of Film Studies, University of Nebraska

facebook Constellations

Constelbooks

Also available in this series

12 Monkeys Susanne Kord

Blade Runner Sean Redmond

Children of Men Dan Dinello

Close Encounters of the Third Kind Jon Towlson

The Damned Nick Riddle

Dune Christian McCrea

Ex Machina Joshua Grimm

Inception David Carter

Mad Max Martyn Conterio

RoboCop Omar Ahmed

Rollerball Andrew Nette

Forthcoming

Jurassic Park Paul Bulloch

Lost Brigid Cherry

Seconds Jez Conolly & Emma Westwood

Stalker Jon Hoel

The Stepford Wives Samantha Lindop

CONSTELLATIONS

Brainstorm

Joseph Maddrey

Acknowledgements

The origin of this project was my friendship with screenwriter Bruce Joel Rubin, who kindly allowed me to review his early notes and scripts for *The George Dunlap Tape*. Except where indicated, all of the quotations from Bruce in this book came from interviews I conducted with him between 2014 and 2016. I am grateful for his time and his friendship. I am also grateful to Douglas Trumbull, the director of *Brainstorm*, and to Philip F. Messina and Robert Stitzel, the credited screenwriters of *Brainstorm*, who shared memories of the project with me during interviews conducted in 2017 and 2018. Furthermore, I am indebted to many journalists and archivists whose research made this book possible. Chief among them: Kyle Counts and Charlotte Wolter of *Cinefantastique* magazine; Tony Crawley and Phil Edwards of *Starburst* magazine; David Hutchison of *Starlog* magazine; Jessie Horsting of *Fantastic Films* magazine; Brad Munson of *Cinefex* magazine; Susan Halpert and Dorothy Borry of the Houghton Library at Harvard University; Rachel Bernstein and Louise Hilton of the Margaret Herrick Library at the Academy of Motion Picture Arts and Sciences. Thanks also to Jon Towlson for encouraging me to write this book, and to John Atkinson for publishing it.

First published in 2020 by
Auteur, an imprint of Liverpool University Press,
4 Cambridge Street, Liverpool L69 7ZU
www.liverpooluniversitypress.co.uk/imprints/Auteur/
Copyright © Auteur 2020

Series design: Nikki Hamlett at Cassels Design
Set by Cassels Design www.casselsdesign.co.uk

All rights reserved. No part of this publication may be reproduced in any material form (including photocopying or storing in any medium by electronic means and whether or not transiently or incidentally to some other use of this publication) without the permission of the copyright owner.

British Library Cataloguing-in-Publication Data
A catalogue record for this book is available from the British Library

ISBN paperback: 978-1-9160842-2-3
ISBN ebook: 978-1-9160842-3-0

Contents

Acknowledgements 4
I. INITIALISING 7
II. GATHERING 11
    Science Fiction and Cinema in the 1950s
    Technology and Consciousness in the 1960s
    Darkness and Enlightenment in the 1970s
III. ASSIMILATING 23
    The George Dunlap Tape (1976 draft)
    The George Dunlap Tape 2.0 (1977 draft)
    Showscan
    The *Star Wars* Effect
    The George Dunlap Tape 3.0 (1978 draft)
    The Dunlap Tapes and *The Light Fantastic* (1979)
    Brainstorm (February 1981 draft)
IV. PRODUCING 47
    Casting and Rehearsals
    Brainstorm (September 1981 drafts)
    Production and Tragedy
    Death and Rebirth
V. STREAMING 67
    The Grid
    The Hat
    The Tape
    Heaven and Hell

VI. EVOLVING 83
    Legacy

    Bright Lights and Tech Noir in the 1980s

    Virtual and Expanded Reality in the 1990s

    The Future is Now

BIBLIOGRAPHY 93

I. INITIALISING

'Imagine a machine that records sights... sounds... sensations, thoughts.... feelings... emotions, even your dreams and nightmares. Then, at the touch of a button, transfers these personal experiences from one mind to another. Any person. Any experience. Anything you can imagine.'

This tantalising blurb appeared on MGM/UA's 1984 VHS release of the film *Brainstorm*, and it is entirely appropriate that the pitch begins and ends with the word 'imagine'. The makers of *Brainstorm* spent more than a decade transferring the revolutionary concept of an 'empathy machine' from page to screen, and since 1984 the film has continued to inspire viewers to imagine possibilities for the future. As a result, *Brainstorm* now seems less like a fixed piece of film history than an idea in evolution. The screen story embodies the ambitions of sci-fi cinema going back to the 1950s, as well as the turbulent culture of the Western world in the 1960s and 1970s. It also foreshadows technological breakthroughs around the turn of the twenty-first century, making the film startlingly relevant to our digitally-enhanced Information Age. So why isn't *Brainstorm* recognised as one of the all-time great science fiction films?

When it was released in US theatres on September 30, 1983, *Brainstorm* was hyped as the boldest genre film since Stanley Kubrick's *2001: A Space Odyssey* (1968). Director Douglas Trumbull—the special effects wunderkind behind *2001*, as well as *Close Encounters of the Third Kind* (1977), *Star Trek: The Motion Picture* (1979) and *Blade Runner* (1982)—promised that it would be nothing less than a revolution of the movie-going experience, saying, 'What we have tried to do is to make a movie that will feel like a dream. You don't simply watch a dream as a passive observer, you fall into its world. A dream surrounds you, and at the same time penetrates at a sensory level. If we've done our job right, you won't simply see *Brainstorm*. You will *feel* it.'[1] Trumbull insisted that *Brainstorm* would raise the bar on cinematic sci-fi spectacle, and also have 'more humanity' than the usual Hollywood fare.[2] This did not seem like an idle boast for a film starring four Oscar-worthy thespians: Christopher Walken, Natalie Wood, Louise Fletcher, and Cliff Robertson. In theory, *Brainstorm* was a perfect fusion of old-fashioned Hollywood glitz and glamour with New Hollywood swagger and special effects.

In reality, it was a cursed project. On November 21, 1981, while on a break from filming, the film's leading lady Natalie Wood tragically drowned off the coast of Catalina Island in southern California. The production was immediately shut down, amid salacious rumors of an affair between Christopher Walken and Natalie Wood (both of whom were married at the time) and the possibility that Wood's death was not an accident. MGM contemplated scrapping the project altogether, but the director managed to convince the studio's insurers to finance completion. It was a remarkable Hollywood ending, but not an entirely triumphant one.

In the fall of 1983, the $18 million movie went out into the world with a whimper instead of a bang. Critics were harsh, and box office returns were modest at best. There were a few exceptional reviews; Stephen Schaefer of US magazine called it a 'landmark movie,' declaring Brainstorm 'as ripely prophetic as 2001, as uniquely visual as anything from George Lucas, as mockingly computer-bemused as WarGames'. Others heaped praise on the cast, and on James Horner's ethereal score. The majority of reviewers, however, expressed disappointment. Many compared the film unfavorably to Ken Russell's recent film Altered States (1980) and to John Badham's WarGames (1983), while some merely dismissed it as an empty-headed light show. In its first seven weeks in limited release, the film reportedly made just over $3 million. Although it would go into wider release in mid-November, and eventually earn another $7 million at the domestic box office, the verdict was in: Brainstorm was a bust.

Screenwriter Bruce Joel Rubin—who had conceived the screen story nearly ten years prior—was dismayed by the tepid response. Speaking to a reporter for his hometown newspaper at the time, he said, 'Not only am I confused, the studio's confused.' He did, however, hold out some hope for the future. Noting that 'the group that seems to be most excited is the youth audience,' the writer suggested that *Brainstorm* might still 'turn out to be the 'trip' movie of the 80s—a *2001* or *Close Encounters—* something that opens up a new dimension' for Generation X.[3]

Once younger viewers began to discover *Brainstorm* on home video, the film did indeed develop a cult following. Screenwriter Robert Stitzel, who wrote the shooting script for the film, remembers: 'Oddly, for a film that was made to be put on the big screen and be a very filmic experience, it made most of its money in videocassettes. That was when people realised for the first time, wow, you can make some real money off of this ancillary market. I remember getting residual checks of $100, $200 from the film [during its theatrical release]. Then, the following Christmas, I got a check for $40,000! Merry Christmas, Bob! And I still get residual checks for that film sometimes.'

Brainstorm's legacy goes beyond the ones and zeroes. Philip F. Messina, who shares screenwriting credit on the finished film, explains, 'I teach directing one day a week at the Academy of Art University in San Francisco. They just formed a Virtual Reality school there, and when one of the people in that department found out that I was teaching there, he said, 'You know, we're talking about *Brainstorm* in our classes.' Which just goes to show that it was way ahead of its time.' Douglas Trumbull cites a comparable experience: 'I got invited to join a company called Magic Leap down in Florida, which is doing probably the most advanced development of virtual reality and augmented, or Mixed Reality system. I went down there to work with their team and met all these young men and women in their twenties—wizard technicians from Cal-Tech and MIT and places like that—and they're all talking about *Brainstorm*. That movie really touched them—the whole concept of altered reality, delivered by some kind of device.' Two decades into the twenty-first century, *Brainstorm* seems to have a second life.

Some viewers began laying the groundwork for this rebirth years ago. In a 1986 article for the *Journal of Humanistic Psychology*, author and scientist Thomas B. Roberts wrote, 'When future historians of cinema look back on Douglas Trumbull's movie *Brainstorm*, what will come to their minds? Will it be the fact that this was Natalie Wood's last movie? Will they think of the struggle director Trumbull had getting MGM to complete and release the film rather than take the insurance money and run? Will they think of the movie and its story?' Although most critical commentaries of the day revolved around Wood's death and Trumbull's fight, Roberts argued that *Brainstorm* should be remembered for 'psycho-critical reasons'—as a pioneering example of science fiction narratives about 'inner space,' offering 'a new, contemporary view of the hero archetype, the Hero as Consciousness Explorer.'[4] That's how the writers of *Brainstorm*—Bruce Rubin, Philip Messina, Robert Stitzel, and Douglas Trumbull—conceived the film, and today it's much easier to view and review the film in that light.

Brainstorm may be a flawed film, but it is nevertheless one of the most intriguing and ambitious Hollywood studio films ever made, and arguably one of the most important science fiction films ever made. To fully appreciate the film's 'ultimate experience,' however, it helps to understand how the film evolved from concept to completion. This book aims to provide context for such an understanding, beginning with a brief history of science fiction cinema and setting up a careful consideration of multiple drafts of the *Brainstorm* screenplay. It will also briefly examine the production history of the film (including the tragic death of star Natalie Wood), the revolutionary career of director and special effects wizard Douglas Trumbull, the particulars of the completed film, and the film's influence on the future of science fiction cinema.

Sit back, relax, and prepare to see *Brainstorm* through new eyes.

Footnotes

1. Horsting 22
2. Farber: 'Brainstorming' 82
3. Dawson
4. Roberts: 'Brainstorm' 126

II. GATHERING

Science Fiction and Cinema in the 1950s

Brainstorm began with a generation of geeks. America's so-called Baby Boomers grew up on a steady diet of fantastic genre films, and Space Age epics like *Destination Moon* (1950), *The Day the Earth Stood Still* (1951) and *When Worlds Collide* (1951) ushered in a golden era of science fiction cinema. Bruce Joel Rubin remembers seeing *When Worlds Collide* for the first time, at the impressionable age of eleven: 'I came out of the theater with a friend named Billy Robinson. We stood on the street corner for hours—I have never in my life stood on a street corner for hours—and just talked about the meaning of it all. It was the beginning of philosophy in my life. It was the beginning of speculation about the awareness of life. It changed me.'[5] As an adult, Rubin continues to believe in the transformative potential of science fiction cinema. 'I think science fiction is a doorway to truth,' he says. 'Because it has very few ground rules, it gives you an opportunity to break out of the concretised world that we all live in. I know some people can't abide it; they can't abide fantasy or science fiction because they only want to be here, in the real world. I have always, in some sense, wanted to be somewhere else. I found this world to be intriguing, but too knowable. The other world was more compelling, and science fiction—especially stories about what the mind really is, and what human beings are capable of—has always fascinated me.'

Douglas Trumbull, born one year before Rubin, had an equally formative childhood experience at the movies—but for him it was the technological spectacle that made the biggest impression. In the early 1950s, Hollywood studios had begun experimenting with new methods for projecting and displaying their films, and innovations like widescreen, multitrack stereo sound, Eastmancolor and 3-D contributed to a more vivid moviegoing experience. Twentieth Century-Fox executive Darryl Zanuck described the emerging blockbusters as 'participatory events,' thereby making a distinction between movies as passive entertainment and movies as recreation. 'Entertainment is something others provide for you,' he explained, 'while recreation is something you provide in some measure for yourself—something in which you participate.'[6] Advertisements for the groundbreaking widescreen process

Promotional art for This is Cinerama! (Cinerama Releasing, 1952)

Cinerama similarly boasted, 'You won't be gazing at a movie screen—you'll find yourself swept right into the picture, surrounded by sight and sound.'[7]

The film *This is Cinerama!* (1952) launched this new trend by presenting widescreen footage of exotic locales in a series of disconnected vignettes. Audiences were dazzled, but some critics worried that the technology would encourage filmmakers to trade narrative integrity for sheer spectacle. Nonetheless, when competitors like CinemaScope and Todd-AO improved upon Cinerama with innovations of their own, the studios (led by Zanuck) spent several years making lavish epics: westerns, war movies, period dramas, and musicals. Trumbull remembers, 'My father made sure I went to every Cinerama movie—so I saw all those movies like *How the West Was Won* (1963) and *The Wonderful World of the Brothers Grimm* (1962), which was not a great movie but it was in the process. And *Windjammer* (1958), which was in another competing process [Cinemiracle] that was actually better than Cinerama. Then came the Todd-AO movies and 70mm larger screens.'

Surprisingly, the major studios did not invest in science fiction epics, with the notable exception of MGM's *Forbidden Planet* (1956). At the time, science fiction cinema was widely regarded as 'kid's stuff'—mostly, a series of cartoonish variations on traditional monster myths. As late as 1959, a respected film critic like *Film Quarterly*'s Richard Hodgens could casually assert that 'to the film audience, 'science fiction' means 'horror,' distinguished from ordinary horror only by a relative lack of plausibility'.[8] Hodgens was not the first or the last critic to bemoan the dumbing-down of serious *literary* science fiction by Hollywood showmen who didn't know droids from Dracula. In 1967, when literary science fiction was entering a new golden age thanks to the 'New Wave' movement in the UK, critic Carlos Clarens reiterated the consensus view that 'for the intellectual speculations of the printed page, the screen substituted color, lots of sound, CinemaScope, special effects, and even the third dimension'. At the same time, however, Clarens cited recent European films like *La Jetée* (1962), *Alphaville* (1965), and *Fahrenheit 451* (1966) as evidence that a new, more philosophical era of science fiction cinema was dawning. He argued that spectacle alone would no longer be enough for fans, and concluded, 'There now seems to be no place [for science fiction cinema] to go except inward.'[9] Boomers like Rubin and Trumbull were more than ready for a fantastic voyage into the human psyche.

Technology and Consciousness in the 1960s

In his 1964 book *Understanding Media: The Extensions of Man*, social theorist Marshall McLuhan prophesied, 'After three thousand years of explosion, by means of fragmentary and mechanical technologies, the Western world is imploding.' He wrote that the present age would soon climax with a 'technological simulation of consciousness, when the creative process of knowing will be collectively and corporately extended to the whole of human society'.[10] The Internet and information technology of the twenty-first century was still science fiction in the mid-1960s, but the idea of a mass awakening into communal consciousness was central to America's counterculture movement between 1964 and 1972.

On the cusp of that transformative era, the 1964/1965 World's Fair in New York heralded a unifying message: 'Peace Through Understanding.' For two consecutive summers, a 646-acre fairground in Queens hosted 150 pavilions representing nearly 70 foreign nations, multiple world religions, and all the top brands of Corporate

America. Sprinkled among the pavilions were dozens of restaurants and concession stands, including one where Bruce Rubin had a summer job selling hot dogs and beer. By then, Rubin was a student at NYU's Film School, studying alongside future talents such as Martin Scorsese, Mike Wadleigh, Jim McBride, and Brian DePalma. On the verge of graduation, however, he was struggling to figure out what kind of stories he might want to tell as a professional filmmaker.

Rubin remembers that on his lunch breaks, he routinely went to the Johnson Wax pavilion's Theater-in-the-Air, to watch Francis Thompson's 18-minute documentary *To Be Alive!* The film was a compilation of footage shot around the world, and intended to illustrate the universality of human experience as it progressed from images of children at play to adult artists at work. *To Be Alive!* concluded with a memorable line of voiceover narration: 'We need never lose our sense of life's wonder, and its joy.' Rubin says that this simple line resonated for him as a profound revelation: 'I knew I wanted to make movies that made people feel like that. I wanted to bring that feeling into the world somehow—that it's an amazing thing to be alive.'

On the other side of the fairgrounds, another mind-bending film was being screened inside the Cinerama dome at the Transportation and Travel pavilion. Director Con Pederson's documentary *To the Moon and Beyond* was a 15-minute, 70mm odyssey that started with a scene of a rocket exploring the vast reaches of outer space, then juxtaposed that broad view of the cosmos with an inward journey through the subatomic material of a human cell. The visual effects, created by a southern California firm called Graphic Films, made a lasting impression on a man in the audience named Stanley Kubrick.

After he saw *To the Moon and Beyond*, Kubrick hired Graphic Films to create concept art and preliminary designs for a feature film he was developing. At the time, the project was known as *Journey Beyond the Stars*. Among the Graphic Films artists who worked on the designs was Douglas Trumbull, a young technical illustrator who had created background art for promotional films for NASA and the United States Air Force. Kubrick was so impressed with Trumbull's work that he hired the artist as a permanent part of the production team on *Journey Beyond the Stars*, which was soon retitled *2001: A Space Odyssey*.

Trumbull remembers, 'That was my film school, working with Stanley Kubrick. And Kubrick was going through this really interesting metamorphosis in his style. He realised that the medium itself had a lot to do with the way he was going to tell the story. The giant screen and the immersive-ness of it all wasn't on his mind when he started making the movie, but he had a realisation that—through the power of Cinerama, and these giant 100-foot-wide screens—he could transport the audience into space, into a kind of virtual reality or flight simulator. After that, he got rid of all the melodrama and over-the-shoulder shots and reverse-angle shots. Imagine Keir Dullea in the pod saying, 'Oh wow, I'm in a light show!' He just got rid of all that crap, because he didn't want it to intrude on the audience's ability to be *in* the movie.'

The theatrical release of *2001: A Space Odyssey* in April 1968 was a high-water mark for Cinerama, maximising the potential of the format. Although some viewers scoffed at the film's untraditional narrative which emphasised theme and visual effects over plot and characterisation, a new wave of film critics like Michel Ciment praised the film on the behalf of the youth audience. Ciment wrote in 1968, 'Kubrick has broken away from the old dramatic framework. Form is content; the film itself is a voyage into space, an experience of the senses.'[11]

2001 was also a watershed moment for science fiction cinema. Following Ciment's lead, film genre historians like John Baxter and John Brosnan contextualised Kubrick's work as a super-western and a religious epic for the rising New Age—in short, the apotheosis of science fiction cinema for a generation that took science fiction seriously and believed in its transformative power. Brosnan wrote that 'Kubrick's aim was to force his audiences [...] to re-examine their own perceptions of the Universe,' and concluded, 'Whether one considers *2001* as a religious epic or as a science fiction film that deals with religious concepts scientifically one has to admit that it succeeds in creating a sense of awe and wonder around the basic mystery of the Universe.'[12]

The most awe-inspiring sequence in the film is a climactic 23-minute audiovisual odyssey entitled 'Jupiter and Beyond the Infinite'. This sequence begins with one of Doug Trumbull's most significant contributions to *2001*—a hypnotic light show generated by a process the effects designer termed 'slit-scan'. By inserting a narrowly-pierced, transparent slide between the moving camera and a moving image, Trumbull created a psychedelic rush of colors at the head of Kubrick's 'ultimate trip'. The results earned the director an Academy Award for Best Visual Effects, and inspired a generation of moviegoers to turn off the lights, relax and float downstream. The final image in *2001*—a moving portrait of a celestial 'star baby'— suggested to viewers that the destiny of the Baby Boomer generation would involve a symbolic rebirth. This oblique message resonated strongly in 1968, when America's counterculture movement was in full force.

*

Like many of his peers, Bruce Rubin was swept up by that counterculture movement, as well as the attendant drug culture. After graduating from NYU in the spring of 1965, he had taken an editing job at NBC and was living in a midtown Manhattan apartment with his friend Barry Kaplan. One day, Rubin remembers, a friend of LSD guru Timothy Leary visited them there: 'He had just arrived in New York to deliver Leary a container of pure LSD from the Sandoz lab in Switzerland. It was about the size of an applesauce jar, and he asked Barry if he could leave it in our refrigerator overnight before he went up to [Leary's home in] Millbrook.' Rubin adds, with a mischievous grin, 'I always tell people that if someone had poured that container into the water supply of New York City, we'd be living in a completely different world today.'

The future screenwriter says he contemplated taking LSD because, at that time, it was the thing to do. 'LSD was *the* drug at that moment in time,' he remembers. 'It hadn't been demonised yet. There were a lot of influential articles talking about this amazing chemical that changed people psychologically—I remember *Look* magazine ran a story about Cary Grant and his experiences with LSD—and I *wanted* to be changed psychologically. I didn't know where it would lead, but I was intrigued by the possibilities.' Kaplan agreed to help his roommate through the trip, using Leary's book *The Psychedelic Experience: A Manual Based on the Tibetan Book of the Dead* as a practical guide. Kaplan also provided a 650-microgram pill for the occasion. Initially, however, the pill had no effect. That's when the two friends remembered the jar of pure LSD in the refrigerator. Rubin says, 'Barry had an eyedropper and he said he would administer a little drop to me.' Instead, his friend accidentally squirted 'a whole syringe of LSD—thousands and thousands of micrograms—down my throat'. Rubin was surprisingly Zen about it. He recalls, 'I said, 'Well, okay'. I mean, what could I do? There was nothing I could do about it. Nowhere to run. All I could do was wait'.

That day in his New York apartment, the writer embarked on an inward space odyssey that seemed to last for thousands of years. He remembers the experience as a timeless journey through a Dantean hell, followed by a total disintegration of personal identity and a complete loss of faith in consensus reality: 'Everything I knew about life was almost immediately destroyed as an idea or a concept. Life as I knew it was gone. At the same time, I was on a journey that was exceedingly familiar. I had a sense that I had done this multiple times before. I was back on a grand journey. In those days, they called it 'the trip'. It was taking me apart and disassembling me on every level. And that process—the deconstruction of the ego-structured mind—was pretty horrifying'. Hours—or what felt like centuries—later, Rubin returned to the world he had formerly taken for granted, and tried to get his bearings. 'I sat there wondering, *Why am I here? Why did I come back?* And a voice answered, 'To tell people what you saw'.'

Rubin's first order of business was to find a language for what he had experienced. Around the same time, Kaplan gave him a copy of the sacred Hindu text *The Bhagavad Gita*. 'If he had given it to me the day before the LSD trip,' Rubin says, 'I would not have understood it at all. But now, I started reading it and I saw everything in a new context.' After that, he discovered Aldous Huxley's 1945 book *The Perennial Philosophy*, a cross-cultural anthology of writings about religious transcendence. For Rubin, Huxley's message came as another revelation: 'Now I know what happened to me. Now I get it. This was a *mystical experience*'.'

But Rubin became troubled about the origins of his experience. 'I felt like a fraud because my experience came from a drug,' he says. Yearning for a more 'authentic' mystical experience, he quit his job at NBC and went searching for the hidden world of saints and mystics. In the summer of 1966, he began a year-long overland journey through Eastern Europe, the Middle East, India, Tibet, East Asia and Japan. Along the way he encountered many spiritual teachers, including Anandamayi Ma (a Hindu sage), the Maharishi Yogi (the founder of Transcendental Meditation, and personal guru to The Beatles), the Guru Maharaj (eventual leader of the Divine Light Mission), and the Dalai Lama. With each encounter, Rubin sensed that he had not yet found what he was looking for. His journey culminated with a visit to a record store in Japan, where he heard Jefferson Airplane's album *Surrealistic Pillow* for the first time. While listening to Grace Slick sing 'Somebody to Love,' he realised that 'the world had changed while I was on my journey, and that everything I was looking for in the Orient was happening in America'. He promptly returned to New York.

There, Rubin found his teacher—a swami named Rudrananda, or 'Rudi' to his friends, who ran an oriental art store in Greenwich Village. Under Rudi's guidance, Rubin began developing a lifelong spiritual practice while also cultivating an 'amorphous career' as a filmmaker. In 1968, he collaborated with friends Brian DePalma and Robert Fiore on the documentary film *Dionysis in '69*, and later worked as an assistant director on DePalma's film *Hi, Mom!* (1970) and several other off-Hollywood projects. He also started writing an original screenplay about the future and fate of the human race—a fable for the 1970s.

Darkness and Enlightenment in the 1970s

In a 1978 interview, Douglas Trumbull reflected, 'We thought at the time that *2001* would start a big trend. It really didn't. Kubrick didn't just jump into making another science-fiction movie, to try and top himself. In fact, *2001* left a huge void... The main effect it had, still has today in fact, is that people look at *2001* and say, 'No one's ever going to do this again. No one's ever going to have the patience, the money or the talent to pull it together.''[13] In fact, Kubrick did make another science fiction movie, but *A Clockwork Orange* (1971) presented a very different vision of the future, full of violent horrors. More reminiscent of 1969's Manson Family murders than 1967's Summer of Love, *Clockwork* accurately reflected a sudden cultural shift toward darker times.

In the short term, the 1968 film *Planet of the Apes* had a much greater influence on sci-fi cinema in the 1970s than did *2001*. The comparatively bleak ending of *Apes*—

Charlton Heston's discovery that he is stranded on Earth in a distant, post-apocalyptic future—inspired a rash of dystopian science fiction films, including *No Blade of Grass* (1970), *The Omega Man* (1971), *Z.P.G.* (1972), and *Soylent Green* (1973). Trumbull couldn't escape the tenor of the times; in 1971 he designed special effects for the technophobic thriller *The Andromeda Strain*. One year later he directed his own post-apocalyptic sci-fi film.

Trumbull says that the initial idea for his directorial debut, *Silent Running* (1972), came from the 1932 horror film *Freaks*. '[*Freaks*] was about a group of sideshow people,' he remembers, 'and one of them was a guy without any legs. He was a good actor and an interesting character. He walked on his hands—it was absolutely incredible. He could stand on one hand and drink from a cup in the other, like a bird perched on a table. And I thought, you could make a robot that way.'[14] With this idea in mind, Trumbull wrote a six-page story treatment about a tree-hugging space cowboy whose closest friends are three robots that help him care for Earth's last remaining forest, housed on the deck of a deep-space freighter. When government agents decide to destroy the forest, the eco-cowboy aligns himself with the machines. Together, they murder his fellow astronauts in order to save the last vestiges of the natural world. To Trumbull, the story conveyed an optimistic message about the potential future relationship between man and machine—but, obviously, it conveyed a less hopeful message about man's relationship to his fellow man.

Initially, Trumbull says, he had no intention of writing or directing the film. Three different writers—Steven Bochco, Deric Washburn and Michael Cimino—fleshed out his original concept, but Trumbull wasn't satisfied with any of their scripts. He eventually decided to craft a shooting script himself by 'cutting their drafts apart and pasting them together with scotch tape and then rewriting it again to clean it up'.[15] After that, Trumbull took over the director's chair, because he felt that there wasn't 'anybody around who was a confident director capable of doing what I wanted to do'.[16] The 29-year-old artist became a filmmaker by default—and *Silent Running* was his crash course.

Around the time that Trumbull was cutting his teeth as a filmmaker, Bruce Rubin was brainstorming a very different vision of the future. His first spec screenplay, co-written with his friend David Bienstock in 1970, was an attempt to create a fictional analogue to his own mystical experience. The screenplay, entitled *Quasar*, revolves around an astronomer named Stuart Townley, whose job is to investigate the source and meaning of quasi-stellar radio signals. Rubin remembers that scientists of the day didn't know exactly what quasars were, and so he took the creative license to imagine what they might be. 'What we're seeing could be the Big Bang,' he theorised. 'It could be the moment of creation itself. And [Stuart Townley] is one of the first people to realise that. What it does for him is what LSD did for me—it gives him a jolt into another version of reality.'

After his initial awakening—an experience comparable to the 'trip' in Kubrick's *2001*—Townley tries to reconcile two worlds: his everyday world and the larger, hidden world of his mystical experience. In the end, the screenwriters suggest, Townley's journey will foreshadow the dawning of a more enlightened form of human consciousness in the Age of Aquarius. Rubin sums up: '*Quasar* was a celebratory prediction that something mystical was going to pervade the culture. It would enter the world, and we would observe it through the journey of that first man. Then, as he started to figure out what it meant—how it was going to change us, what we were going to become as a civilization—a group of people would have the same experience. It was a very utopian story, very enthusiastic about what the world could be.'

Unfortunately, *Quasar* was never made. Ingo Preminger, producer of the hit film *M*A*S*H* (1970), optioned Rubin and Bienstock's script but then couldn't convince his producing partners to finance the project. The special effects requirements written into the script were simply too daunting, so *Quasar*'s death was a matter of money. Rubin reflects, 'It wasn't made because it was a $9 million film.' The writer took the lesson to heart and started working on a new script that would tackle the same basic idea 'in a smaller way and with a smaller budget'.

At the heart of his new script, begun in 1973 and continually revised over the next three years, was the concept of a device that would allow people to record and share their most intimate experiences, as well as their deepest thoughts and feelings. The concept presupposed that every human mind is, on some level, comprised of tangible information that can be stored and retrieved. In essence: We are walking, talking computers. It was a timely idea—one that would become popular in the literary science fiction community during the second half of the decade. In 1975, author Philip K. Dick theorised that 'each one of us is a vast storage drum of taped information'.[17] A year later, he wrote an influential essay ('Man, Android and Machine') proposing that information itself is alive, and we are all terminals in a giant super-computer. New Wave author J.G. Ballard espoused a similar notion around the same time, arguing that new media—everything from Hollywood movies to Madison Avenue ads—has substituted a largely fictional landscape for conventional reality. Ballard envisioned a future in which everything we experience is recorded and played back—not just for entertainment, but for enlightenment. In a 1979 interview, he offered this vision of the future: 'Instead of having to watch the news as transmitted by the BBC or ITV—that irrelevant mixture of information about a largely fictional external world—one will be able to sit down, relax and watch the *real* news. And the real news of course will be a computer-selected and computer-edited version of the day's rushes. 'My God, there's Jenny having her first ice cream!' or 'There's Candy coming home from school with her new friend'.' Ballard suggested that new technology might thereby allow human beings to transcend time, and overcome 'the awful finiteness of life'.[18]

With his second script *The George Dunlap Tape*, Bruce Rubin had already imagined such a future—but in his mind the key to transcendence was not the ability to replay one's own experiences, but the ability to share those personal experiences with others. Rubin's spiritual teacher Rudi once said that 'in your search for enlightenment you must be able to see situations from as many vantage points as possible.'[19] In Rubin's script, new technology facilitates that goal—allowing individuals to access a database of infinite human memories from any terminal at any time. The revolution, Rubin promised, would be televised.

Footnotes

5. Bauer 34-35
6. Belton 77
7. Belton 189
8. Hodgens 79
9. Clarens 162
10. McLuhan 3
11. Ciment 140
12. Brosnan 177
13. Crawley: 'Wizard' 35
14. Anderson 12
15. Bozung
16. Kermode 11
17. Dick 129
18. Ballard
19. Rudi 62

III. ASSIMILATING

The George Dunlap Tape (1976 Draft)

According to Bruce Rubin's 1976 synopsis, '*The George Dunlap Tape* is a science fiction story of a scientist inventor who, while employed by a giant multi-national telephone and communications corporation, invents a tape recorder which can record and play back the full sensatory range of the human brain: sight, sound, smell, taste, feeling, memories, the future, the afterlife. Transcribed by computer and laser technology, the multi-sensory tape recorder opens whole new vistas of human experience. It allows man, for the first time, to totally enter another man's experience—to become quarterback for the Rams, explore the undersea worlds, eat in the best restaurants—without ever leaving his easy chair and his multi-sensory hookup. It is a fountain of youth, of wisdom and terror for those whose experiments with the machine provide the basis for the film.'

Rubin's early screenplay begins with a short, impressionistic preview of the life of George Dunlap, inventor of this revolutionary 'tape recorder'. The story fast-forwards through moving images of his conception, birth, and childhood to arrive at the present day, in which the 40-ish scientist is testing his invention inside a lab at the ICT Research Center. The test is successful: Dunlap's colleague Richard Abramson uses a custom-designed helmet to play back a multi-sensory recording of Dunlap's experience of walking down a hallway and pausing to smell a woman's perfume. After the test, Abramson touts the revolutionary possibilities of the invention to ICT head honcho Robert Rankill, while Dunlap goes home to his wife Ruth and two young children, Mark and Amy.

In subsequent scenes, both Rankill and Mark Dunlap test the machine by playing back pre-recorded tapes. Rankill is wildly enthusiastic, and begins speculating about practical applications—everything from training airline pilots to treating schizophrenia. Mark's test, on the other hand, offers the first glimmer of danger. The 8-year-old boy learns to drive by watching one of his father's tapes, and then takes the family car for an illicit late-night spin. He crashes the car, but luckily escapes injury.

Undaunted, Abramson conducts his own private tests with shared-reality porn. His experiences lead him to question the nature of his own existence. The screenwriter explains that this sequence illustrated the most important question in the story: 'If we can be someone else in their experiential space, then *who are we?* What, really, is the thing that is living these experiences?'

George Dunlap asks the same question when he learns that his invention can transfer conscious thought as well as sensory experience. Later, while reviewing a tape made by his wife Ruth, he realises that the machine can also record *unconscious* thoughts. This poses another important question: *Can two people still love each other if they know each other's deepest, darkest thoughts?* The screenwriter's implied answer is yes; George Dunlap regards his invention as a means of bringing people closer together, and that's exactly what it does for him and his wife.

Of course, not everyone is so optimistic. The script introduces a character named Jerry Zimbach, a watchdog for the U.S. Department of Commerce. When Zimbach learns about the invention, he theorises that it could have a major impact on society. If people become addicted to shared-reality entertainment, he worries, they might start to abandon conventional reality—stop going to work, stop paying attention to laws, stop eating, stop doing all the things that hold civilization together. George Dunlap's machine could actually cause the end of the world as we know it. With this in mind, Zimbach employs a spy named Michael Evans to steal Dunlap's research from ICT and destroy all existing prototypes of the invention.

Meanwhile, Dunlap continues to explore advanced applications of his invention. His terminally-ill mother-in-law Laura implores him to make a tape-recording of her death, which he does. When the inventor plays back the 'death tape,' hoping to learn what happens when we die, the experience thoroughly convinces him that life does not end when the mind and body cease to function.

Dunlap keeps exploring, and discovers that he can also use his invention to manipulate time. Based on this evidence, he concludes that his entire life already exists somewhere on a pre-recorded tape. He then realises that the whole of human history is stored in a vast super-computer, and that all experiential information— everything every human has ever thought, felt or done—is accessible to any individual at any time. The future is likewise stored in this matrix of information, and can be accessed and viewed just as easily as the past. When Dunlap dares to look ahead, he sees Michael Evans murdering him.

Naturally, Dunlap has some trouble accepting the idea that his life is merely a recording. Because he has seen the future, however, he knows what will happen next. Multiple instances of déjà vu convince him that his life is indeed about to be cut short. Dunlap then uses his invention to transfer all of his recorded thoughts and experiences to his wife Ruth—essentially creating a backup copy of his mind. He then confronts Michael Evans, destroying ICT's computers and both prototypes of his invention in the process. The confrontation ends with his own death.

At the end of the screenplay, George Dunlap's spirit is absorbed into the mysterious white light of the afterlife, and his backup 'tape'—which contains the ultimate truth about the illusionary nature of human existence—resides in the mind of his widow. Ruth resolves to share this truth with the world. The final scene reveals a god-like super-computer—buried deep below the New Mexico desert—simultaneously playing all the tapes that make up humanity's past and future, continually spinning a web of illusionary reality.

Bruce Rubin says he did not intend for the ending to espouse a determinist philosophy. Instead, he regarded this plot twist as a sci-fi analogue to esoteric teachings about the 'Akashic Record'. In early research notes for his script, Rubin wrote, 'The machine is the collective mind, all intelligence. It is the Akashic record, the history of the past, the present and the future.' The term 'Akasa,' a Vedic Sanskrit word for infinite space, was adopted in the late 1800s by occultist and Theosophy founder Helena Blavatsky, who equated it with the concept of a world-soul. Psychologist Carl Jung later incorporated the same concept into his theory of the 'collective unconscious'. In a 1938 essay, Jung wrote, 'It would be a difficult task to reconcile the picture I have of myself with the one which other people have of me. Who is right? And who is the real individual? If we go further and consider the fact that man is also what neither he himself nor other people know of him—an unknown something which can yet be proved to exist—the problem of identity becomes more difficult still.'[20]

This elaboration helps to explain the identity crisis suffered by Richard Abramson in *The George Dunlap Tape*. For Abramson and other characters in the film, Dunlap's invention strips away the illusion of individuality (the ego) and reveals the existence of a world-soul or Akashic record. By recognising that such a record exists, Rubin insists, man can potentially escape it. Adopting classical Judeo-Christian terminology, he proposes that by surrendering individuality and embracing a world-soul, we escape 'Hell' and experience 'Heaven'. To explain: 'Hell is the interminable imprisonment in the bowels of the machine, consciousness locked up in darkness. Life is the possibility of release. Heaven is the return to the Collective Consciousness.'

To his credit, Rubin realised this was heady stuff for a mainstream feature film, but he took some encouragement from the success of recent films like *THX-1138* (1970), *Slaughterhouse Five* (1971) and *Solaris* (1972), all of which challenged audiences to question the world around them. In a 1974 article published in the *New York Times*, science fiction novelist Arthur Herzog declared that this new breed of science fiction films was a vital response to a 'weary' America 'bombarded by daily reports about inflation, pollution and corruption in high places'. Defending the genre against charges of mindless escapism, Herzog concluded that 'no other art form is as well equipped to focus upon the destiny which lies out there on the edges of science and society'.[21] Rubin concurred, and used Herzog's essay to help raise financing to make *The George Dunlap Tape* as an independent feature film.

Left: Bruce Joel Rubin and the IU cyclotron, photo courtesy of Bruce Joel Rubin. Right: The crew of The George Dunlap Tape, photo courtesy of Bruce Joel Rubin

The project came alive when a group of real estate developers in Bloomington, Indiana—where Rubin was living at the time—agreed to put up $400,000. Working under the banner of Aeneid Films, Rubin got to work. He remembers, 'We rented an office. We started scouting locations. We broke down the script. Made a budget. Started building sets. We got permission from the Science Department at Indiana University to shoot inside one of their labs. They had a brand-new cyclotron there. I had a friend who was a pilot, and he was going to shoot aerial shots of the campus. I started casting. I went to Chicago and auditioned people for two or three days. We got some amazingly good actors. Everything was working until, all of the sudden, the investors pulled out. We were one week away from shooting.'

Although his dream of making *The George Dunlap Tape* was temporarily shattered, Rubin didn't give up. In November 1975, he mailed copies of his shooting script to several independent film producers, including former NYU classmate Joel L. Freedman. Freedman, who had already produced two award-winning documentaries (1970's *Skezag* and 1975's *Battle at Treaty Mountain*), optioned the script in late 1976. With Rubin's consent, he then hired frequent collaborator Philip Messina to do a rewrite, in hopes of making Rubin's wildly ambitious story more palatable to Hollywood.

The George Dunlap Tape 2.0 (1977 Draft)

'Bruce and I knew each other at NYU film school,' Messina remembers, 'but we didn't know each other very well until Joel optioned *The George Dunlap Tape* and asked me to read it. I did, and I said, *Wow, this could be a great movie.*' Although captivated by the story, Messina saw room for improvement. 'The characterisations and the structure of the story were somewhat underdeveloped,' he explains. 'My job was to address those issues. I made it an accessible story about universal themes.'

Messina's initial draft of *The George Dunlap Tape*, written in 1977, opens in a movie theater, where an audience is awaiting a mysterious broadcast. God-like voices from the theater's projection booth inform them that the broadcast will be streamed live to theaters around the world. After a few other preliminary remarks, a woman named Ruth Dunlap appears on the movie screen. She wears a strange helmet, and begins sharing her story via a direct transmission of motion pictures from her mind into the minds of the audience. Messina explains, 'What we're watching is the story of George Dunlap's life.'

The story proper starts in a laboratory at ICT, where George is using his invention to transmit sensory experiences to his colleague Richard Abramson. As in Rubin's script, the inventor then goes home to his wife Ruth and two children, 9-year-old Mark and 5-year-old Amy, but new dialogue reveals that the Dunlaps' marriage has become strained because the absent-minded inventor is constantly prioritising work over family.

Subsequent scenes introduce Robert Rankill, the CEO of ICT, and Jerry Zimbach, an undersecretary for the U.S. Department of Commerce, and also add a bit more science to the story's science fiction. A new scene in which Rankill unveils the invention to his fellow ICT board members—allowing them to vicariously experience an array of pre-recorded scenarios, ranging from a night in a Persian harem to a front row seat at a Rolling Stones concert— includes important dialogue about how the tapes can be transmitted to customers 'through the phone lines,' like today's host-based video games. According to Messina, this idea arose from first-hand research: 'Nowadays it's an easy thing to assume: Everything comes through the Internet. Back then, it was a little bit of a new idea. I went to Bell Labs, and they showed me how they were transmitting images from one computer to another, over phone lines. That was the big new thing. Nowadays you get your picture instantly, but back then it took forever. The image went across the screen in horizontal strips while the picture was being transferred.'

In contrast to Rubin's script, which emphasises the revolutionary possibilities of this new technology, Messina's script amplifies the potential dangers. When Richard Abramson becomes addicted to shared-reality sex tapes and suffers an apparent nervous breakdown, Jerry Zimbach delivers the news to Senator James Addison, with a warning that the device could be used as a weapon in psychological warfare. Soon after that, Addison learns something that even the inventor doesn't know: his invention is *already* being developed as a weapon, by a mysterious partner company called Jenco.

Dunlap himself learns this terrifying truth when his mother-in-law dies and he reviews her death tape. What he sees—from his mother-in-law's omniscient POV—is a haunting vision of a future in which Rankill betrays him, and government agents come to kill him. Dunlap also sees a more distant future in which the U.S. government takes complete control of his invention, and uses it to subjugate and even surgically-modify its citizens. These actions prompt a wide-scale revolution that ends in nuclear annihilation of the entire human race. All that's left behind is a series of recorded tapes, stored on a super-computer in an underground bunker.

Once Dunlap recovers from the shock of this apocalyptic vision, he does some research and learns more about Jenco. On a home computer linked to ICT's mainframe, he discovers that his partners have been making tapes to administer torture, interrogation, and mind-control. Before he has time to react, his 4-year-old daughter Amy plays back one of the torture tapes, and experiences an intense nightmare that the screenwriter compares to Hieronymus Bosch's depiction of Hell. The experience leaves her psychologically damaged.

At this point, Rankill restricts the inventor's access to his invention, and Dunlap runs away with his family. Knowing that he will eventually be hunted down, he schemes with his wife to remotely access ICT's computers and transfer his evidence into her mind. After his death, Ruth will play back the tape for the whole world to see.

In the final pages of Messina's screenplay, George Dunlap confronts a government assassin *Matrix*-style, literally dodging a bullet (because he has seen the future, he knows what's coming) and completing his mission. This experience proves to him that it is possible to change the future; if he can evade death, then perhaps Ruth can help prevent the nuclear holocaust. Unfortunately, there is another bullet with George Dunlap's name on it. A second agent shoots and kills him, and Messina's script culminates with a brief vision of George Dunlap 'going into the light'.

Armed with this revised draft, producer Joel Freedman began sending *The George Dunlap Tape* around Hollywood, looking for collaborators. One person he approached was Douglas Trumbull, who responded enthusiastically to the material. 'I was trying to find a project that dealt with the issue of perception,' Trumbull remembers, 'and I felt the script offered that opportunity.'[22]

Showscan

Ever since he made *Silent Running*, Trumbull had been struggling to get a second film off the ground. Numerous projects—including 'an end-of-the-world movie' called *The Pyramid* for MGM, *The Ride* ('about a futuristic theme park ride that takes over people's interest in media and destabilises the social fabric') for Warner Brothers, and *Journey of the Oceanauts* (an underwater version of *2001*) for Twentieth Century-Fox—had fallen by the wayside.[23] In 1974 the filmmaker realised that 'you can't live on development deals,' and decided to pitch something different. He remembers, 'I talked Paramount Pictures into forming this company called Future General Corporation, which was a research and development company to look at the future of cinema technology.'[24]

FGC, a subsidiary of Paramount managed by Trumbull, began conducting tests on film formats, cameras, lenses, and projectors. One of the company's most significant discoveries during this time was related to frame rate projection. Early Hollywood filmmakers had learned that moviegoers can process no more than 10 to 12 images per second *as separate images*, and that higher frame rates create the illusion of a 'motion picture'. Since the late 1920s, 24 frames-per-second had been the standard frame rate for all Hollywood films. This remained true in the 1970s, when Trumbull decided to challenge the norm.

The filmmaker remembers, 'One thing no one had ever tried was to really dramatically change frame rates. [So] we shot films at 24, 36, 48, 66 and 72 frames per second and showed them in a special theater' at California State Polytechnic University. In a test environment, audience members wore sensors on their bodies to document the effects of the higher frame rate projections. 'We did a series of psychological and neurological tests—EKG, EEG, galvanic skin and muscle response—on subjects as we showed them identical movies shot and produced in different frame rates. We found that when you get up to 60 or 70 fps, as it starts approaching [the speed at which the eye perceives] reality, there's a whole new response level.'[25]

Based on the results, Trumbull invented and patented a production and exhibition process called Showscan. In this process, movies would be shot on 65mm film at 60 frames per second, then projected on 70mm film at a rate of 60 frames per second, using higher-than-usual illumination. The result, according to Trumbull, is that 'the surface of the screen just disappears and you feel as if you're looking through a window onto real life'.[26] In a 1978 interview, he explained: 'With ordinary movies, the audience is a third person voyeur, watching some other activity. They get involved intellectually or emotionally in some event through the mechanism of the plot, but in order to *really*, *fully* experience something as though you were there it has to be a hell of an emotional experience. It has to be huge screen, and it has to be believable, real. The sound has to have sound pressure levels that are close to reality. It has to really get you going.'[27] In essence, Trumbull was building a next-generation Cinerama.

Initially, the filmmaker planned to feature the Showscan technology in amusement parks, but his backers at Paramount said they wanted to adopt the process as a new Hollywood filmmaking model. With that in mind, Trumbull sought additional financing to create a fully-equipped movie production studio that could produce a series of 'visual event movies'.[28] Unfortunately, around the same time, Paramount Pictures underwent a corporate restructuring. According to the filmmaker, the new executives were not as eager to support in his new process, which would inevitably require substantial investment in more film stock and larger film prints, and necessitate a major upgrade of screens and projectors in theaters around the world. Responding to their lack of enthusiasm, Trumbull says he tried to leave Paramount and develop Showscan independently, but was unable to get out of his contract and suddenly found himself 'sitting around, twiddling my thumbs and collecting a paycheck'.[29]

The filmmaker's restlessness abated somewhat in 1977, when Paramount agreed to loan him out to rival studio Columbia Pictures, to design the visual effects for Steven Spielberg's new movie *Close Encounters of the Third Kind*. Trumbull did not want to work as an effects supervisor again, but the subject matter of Spielberg's film intrigued him, and he hoped the loan-out deal would help him raise money for a new production studio.

After completing work on *Close Encounters*, Trumbull was still unable to get a second movie off the ground. While he was trying to develop a freewheeling adaptation of Sterling Lanier's post-apocalyptic novel *Hiero's Journey*, producer Joel Freedman approached him with *The George Dunlap Tape*. Trumbull immediately recognised similarities between Dunlap's invention and his own innovations, and decided that Rubin and Messina's story could be the perfect vehicle for Showscan.

'I told Freedman I'd like to direct the film,' Trumbull remembers, 'but he said: 'No, no, no. I don't want you to *direct* the film. I want you to do the special effects.' Frustrated by the limited offer, Trumbull tried to buy the script outright, but the producer wasn't selling. According to Trumbull, Freedman kept searching for a director, while he waited and hoped the project would come back around. As it turned out, he didn't have to wait long.

The *Star Wars* Effect

With a total box office revenue topping $2.3 billion, *Variety* magazine proclaimed 1977 'the biggest year in film history'. George Lucas's film *Star Wars* (1977) accounted for nearly 10% of the entire market, and in November it became the highest-grossing film of all time with a take of more than $120 million.[30] That same month, Steven Spielberg launched his own science fiction epic, *Close Encounters of the Third Kind*. By the end of the year it had grossed $20 million in ticket sales, and would continue its meteoric rise in 1978.

The effects of this box office bonanza were far-reaching and long-lasting. In addition to launching the era of the Hollywood summer blockbuster, Lucas and Spielberg inaugurated a renaissance in science fiction cinema, redefining the popular perception of the genre. Film historian John Kenneth Muir writes that prior to 1977 'the genre concerned what America saw when it gazed into the abyss,' offering consistently bleak visions of the future, while afterward 'the genre was about the country retreating, full-speed from that abyss, and purposefully directing its gaze and attention elsewhere'.[31] Film historian Vivian Sobchack elaborates on the apparent optimism of the new age: 'Through some strange new transformation, technological wonder had become synonymous with domestic hope; space and time seemed to expand again, their experience and representation becoming what can only be called 'youthful'.'[32] Instead of echoing real-world malaise, filmmakers were turning to the stars and dreaming of better worlds. In many ways, it was a return to the zeitgeist of the early 1950s, when science fiction cinema was mostly about spectacle and escapism.

George Lucas proudly admitted that *Star Wars* was a throwback. 'I didn't want to make a *2001*,' he explained in a 1977 interview. 'I wanted to make a space fantasy that was more in the genre of Edgar Rice Burroughs; the whole other end of space fantasy that was there before science took it over in the 1950s.' With *Star Wars*, Lucas claimed he was aiming for the type of 'speculative fiction' that remembers 'the fairy-tales'.[33] *Close Encounters of the Third Kind* demonstrates an equally enchanted worldview. Film critic Pauline Kael summed up Spielberg's message in a single, sarcastic sentence: 'God is up there in a crystal-chandelier spaceship, and He likes us.' She described *Close Encounters* as 'spiritual cotton candy'.[34] Spielberg wasn't inclined to argue; in a 1977 interview, he said, 'It's strictly an entertainment film. I'm not out to educate the country or enlighten people, or make them reason any differently, but I would like them to look up in the sky a little differently, and with a little more curiosity and open-mindedness.'[35]

Douglas Trumbull, right, directs Christopher Walken and Natalie Wood on the set of Brainstorm (MGM/UA, 1983)

Doug Trumbull (who had designed Spielberg's 'crystal-chandelier spaceship') shared the director's attitude and, with the phenomenal success of *Close Encounters*, his own star rose again in Hollywood. Around the same time that Spielberg hailed Trumbull as 'the next Walt Disney,' producer Joel Freedman returned with *The George Dunlap Tape*.[36] Trumbull reflects, 'I don't know what it was that *Close Encounters* did to him, but at that point he decided I was the right person. I said great.'[37]

The George Dunlap Tape 3.0 (1978 Draft)

In early 1978, Trumbull began working with Freedman and Messina on a new draft of the script for Paramount Pictures. In the post-*Star Wars* era, it no longer seemed wise to build the main conflict around a vision of dystopian future or the threat of nuclear annihilation. Messina explains, 'You've got to understand the historical context. After Spielberg did *Jaws* and Lucas did *Star Wars*, it wasn't possible to have a tragic ending anymore. The studios didn't want tragedy.'

Messina's second draft begins with Ruth Dunlap delivering her murdered husband's story to the director of the National Academy of Sciences, amid a flurry of activity. Messina recalls, 'You don't know what's going on. You're getting little snippets of information. Something just happened, somebody died, and the guy says, 'What's this all about?'' The tone suggests that *The George Dunlap Tape* might be a techno-paranoia thriller—something along the lines of *The Parallax View* (1974), *Three Days of the Condor* (1975) or *All the President's Men* (1976)—but this intro turns out to be mostly window dressing for a mythopoetic hero's journey. Messina continues, 'She opens up this little briefcase and there's this recording device inside, and she says, 'Put this on.' Then the screen changes, and what we're watching is what he's watching. It's the story of George Dunlap's life.'

The next scene follows Messina's previous draft, but introduces a new supporting character named Lillian Reynolds, a colleague of George Dunlap and a close family friend. Subsequent scenes establish a new threat, with Rankill warning Dunlap that the Department of Defense will be interested in his invention. Messina recalls that this plot point seemed unavoidable at the time: 'I did a lot of research, and realised that the D.O.D. would have immediately classified an invention like that. That's what they do; they work hand-in-hand with the big tech industries, and anything that has military applications, they can classify it. Of course, companies don't want their inventions classified, because they want to be able to make money off of them.' This sets up the central conflict in the story—a three-way power struggle between George Dunlap, Robert Rankill, and James Zimbach, director of the National Security Agency.

In earlier drafts, George Dunlap tested the potential of his invention by recording his mother-in-law's death. The new draft instead follows Lillian Reynolds into the undiscovered country, and presents her death experience in elaborate visual detail. Messina remembers that the subject of near-death experiences (NDEs) was 'in the air' when he wrote the draft, due the popularity of recent publications like *Life After Life* and *Reflections on Life After Life* by Raymond A. Moody (published in 1975 and 1977, respectively), *At the Hour of Death* by Karlis Osis and Erlendur Haraldsson (1977), and *The Human Encounter with Death* by Stanislav Grof and Joan Halifax (1977). These books presented case studies of NDEs and identified the most commonly-reported visual features of the experiences: a tunnel of energy, a celestial city of light, and what Moody describes as 'a panoramic, wrap-around, full-color, three-dimensional vision of the events of their lives.'[38]

An equally significant influence on Messina's second draft was the writer's own religious background. 'I grew up in the Catholic Church,' he explains. 'When I was ten years old, I said a rosary every night. It was intense. I later broke away from it, but having been a serious Catholic was no small thing in my life. These were important concepts to me. They weren't just movie ideas. I think that's why Bruce and I were such a great combination. The story flowed out of Bruce from his own deep experience. When I came in, it flowed out of my deep experience as well.'

When Dunlap finally plays back Lillian's death tape via a telephone connection to the ICT lab, he witnesses a rush of moving images from Lillian's life, followed by a blinding white light and an otherworldly scream. At that point he realises an important truth: his colleague's life didn't stop when her biological functions ceased. Overwhelmed, the scientist stops playing the tape. By the time he resumes watching it, government spies have tapped into his phone line. A new character named William Jenkins (a less overtly sinister version of Michael Evans) leads the spy operation, and a lab tech named Robertson dies mysteriously when he links himself to Dunlap's feed and views the entirety of Lillian's death tape.

George Dunlap, meanwhile, bypasses the physical effects of sharing the death experience so that he can view the tape without dying. When he plays the tape to the end, he passes through a tunnel of energy and descends into a larger repository of moving images. Dunlap then quickly realises that he is not only viewing fragments of Lillian's life, but reviewing and previewing the experiences of every human being that has ever lived or will ever live. In this grand holographic mainframe of information, Dunlap previews his own personal future—including a confrontation with a demonic-looking Rankill, and his own assassination.

Much of the third act remains the same. George's son, rather than his daughter, experiences the nightmare theater of his father's weaponised invention—a symbolic drowning in a primordial pool filled with archetypal monsters. Later, while the boy is recovering from the experience in a hospital ward, George and Ruth successfully hack into ICT's mainframe and destroy the lab. Government agents finally catch up to George, and the inventor willfully sacrifices himself in order to liberate his invention and safeguard an as-yet-unseen future. Because he is linked with his wife via a phone line at the moment of his death, Ruth shares her husband's experience of life after life. Messina's script details the final stage of the hero's journey in familiar visual terms: a white light, a life-review, a tunnel of energy, and ethereal visions of heavenly beings. As the audio-visual symphony reaches its crescendo, the writer returns to the wraparound story. The director of the National Academy of Sciences stops playing the George Dunlap tape, and stares at Ruth in silent awe.

Rubin campaigned for the restoration of his original epilogue, but he was fighting a losing battle. Luckily, he knew that Messina's script improved the story in terms of characterisation and conflict, and elevated the project as a whole. Trumbull, however, still believed that the script represented 'two or three movies worth of content,' and needed to be further streamlined. Messina reflects, 'I began to have an uneasy feeling that Doug didn't really get the script, in the deepest sense. But, you know, when you're young and ambitious, you hope for the best. You don't listen to those things. It's *Doug Trumbull, Academy Award nominee*! It's *Paramount Pictures, man*! Let's get this great movie made!' After two years of writing and re-writing, Messina believed that *The George Dunlap Tape* was 'hot as a pistol' at Paramount. In fact, he was so confident that he decided to move from New York to Los Angeles to advance his career as a screenwriter. Soon after that, he says, 'my script was thrown out'.

The Dunlap Tapes and *The Light Fantastic* (1979)

The George Dunlap Tape might not have moved forward at all if not for the first big-budget voyage of the Starship Enterprise. In early 1979, *Star Trek: The Motion Picture* was stalled in post-production due to problems with the special effects. According to Trumbull, '[The special effects team] tried to do computer graphics prematurely. The technology was not there to do that. They believed they could make it happen, but they didn't. They spent something like $3 million and didn't have one shot completed. It just looked like it wasn't going to work.'

In the spring, Paramount asked Trumbull to take over the effects work. According to Trumbull, the studio had already accepted an advance payment of $30 million from theatrical exhibitors, and guaranteed the release of *Star Trek* on December 7, 1979—so the film needed to be completed and delivered on a very tight schedule. This put Trumbull in a strong bargaining position, and he agreed to accept the job—on one condition. He wanted to be released from his long-term contract with Paramount as soon as *Star Trek* was finished. He laid out his terms as follows: 'I will do it, but only if I can leave immediately after. Then I'll take [*The George Dunlap Tape*], I'll take Showscan, I'll take my company and be out of my contract.'[39] The deal was made.

Around the same time, Trumbull made his own revisions to the *George Dunlap* script. In the Turner / MGM Scripts collection at the Margaret Herrick Library in Beverly Hills, there is a draft entitled *The Dunlap Tapes*—dated May 4, 1979—that is credited to Bruce Rubin, Philip F. Messina, and Douglas Trumbull. It opens with a longer laboratory scene that more fully illustrates the capabilities of George's invention: the scientist and his colleagues perform sensory tests on each of the five senses, then playfully link the mind of the inventor to a literal lab monkey, adding some humour and levity to the mix. Going forward, Messina's screen story remains mostly intact, although there is added emphasis on the conflict between Dunlap's idealistic goals and the government's secret campaign for a new weapon.

The biggest changes to the script appear in the last forty pages. Instead of a bullet-dodging encounter with a government agent, George Dunlap leads two government agents on a high-speed car chase. Psychedelic flashes of color appear in the hero's field of vision and foreshadow a fatal crash. At the moment of impact, George Dunlap's body stops but his disembodied point-of-view keeps going—forward and up, past the clouds, above the earth, into the dark void of outer space. What comes next is an effects-driven finale that was clearly intended to rival the Star Gate sequence in *2001* as well as the 'crystal-chandelier' Mothership in *Close Encounters of the Third Kind*.

Through George's astral body POV, the audience would experience a rapid-fire life-review, followed by a strobing light show and an audio overload. Then, abruptly, darkness and silence. A white light would appear at the end of a dark tunnel, followed by a series of fragmented visions that the script writer describes in three distinct stages. The first stage was intended to illustrate the vastness of outer space, with a vision of countless stars pulling back to reveal countless galaxies. The second stage would invert the journey, and the macrocosmic universe give way to a microscopic universe—a transition reminiscent of *To the Moon and Beyond*. The third stage would be more abstract, populated by crystalline forms and ethereal music. Finally, the psychedelic journey would end abruptly and the film conclude with a computer readout of the title and production credits.

Once Trumbull completed the effects for *Star Trek*, he pitched *The Dunlap Tapes* and his Showscan process to David Begelman, president and CEO of MGM. Trumbull and Begelman had a strong rapport based on their work together on *Close Encounters of the Third Kind*, but Begelman purportedly regarded the combination of an effects-heavy film and a costly new production/projection process as too much of a gamble. According to Trumbull, the studio exec did 'serious studies of the feasibility of shooting the helmet or 'point-of-view' or 'mind-trip' parts of [*The Dunlap Tapes*] in Showscan, but found himself in a chicken-and-egg situation. The studio wouldn't make the film in Showscan unless exhibitors promised to install the hardware necessary to show it, and exhibitors wouldn't put in the hardware unless guaranteed a steady stream of Showscan films.'[40]

Minus the complications of the Showscan process, however, Begelman offered to help Trumbull make his movie. Trumbull immediately hatched a new plan: 'I came up with the idea of doing [the film] in both 70mm and 35mm. In movies people often do flashbacks and point-of-view shots as a gauzy, mysterious, distant kind of image. And I wanted to do just the opposite, which was to make the material of the mind even more real and more high impact than 'reality'.'[41]

Trumbull's idea was essentially a throwback to the experimental days of early Hollywood, when several major studios shot portions of their most ambitious films in larger formats to dazzle audiences. According to film historian John Belton, these early experiments had an unintended effect on the way audiences perceived widescreen technology. Because the abrupt shift from a smaller-screen format to a larger-screen format 'foregrounded the technology as a novelty' instead of presenting it to audiences as the new normal, widescreen cinema all but disappeared for nearly three decades.[42]

Trumbull might have anticipated this effect on audiences. Certainly, that would account for his stated desire to ground the spectacle of his film in a relatable human story, to keep viewers emotionally engaged. With that in mind, he sought a new screenwriter to punch up the script's characterisations and dialogue, just as he himself had punched up the spectacular finale. Enter Robert Getchell, who was riding high on two recent Oscar nominations—one for his first original screenplay *Alice Doesn't Live Here Anymore* (produced in 1974), and one for his first adapted screenplay *Bound for Glory* (produced in 1976).

Getchell's draft—entitled *The Light Fantastic* and dated January 18, 1980—completely removes the espionage / conspiracy elements of Messina's story and replaces them with an intricate family melodrama. Getchell renames most of the characters, redefines many of the interpersonal relationships, and adds some new characters to complicate the dynamics. George Dunlap becomes Grady Martin, an absent-minded professor whose workaholism has already destroyed one relationship (to his ex-wife Ellen) and is now threatening to destroy another (to girlfriend Carol Jarman). Carol yearns for romantic gestures—flowers and balloons and a trip to Tahiti—but Grady remains consumed by his work.

Both Grady and Carol work for a company called Foursome Toys; Grady in development and Carol in marketing. Foursome Toys also employs Midge Collister, Grady's former mother-in-law and closest confidant, as well as a trio of dopey executives named Bill Meadows, Andy Patterson, and Chris Breed. When Grady expresses concerns about the potentially dangerous side effects of his invention—preliminary studies suggest that using it could be more addictive than using heroin—the trio plans to murder him in order to protect their company's bottom line. After Midge records her own death, they kidnap Grady and force him to watch the death tape in the hope that it will kill him.

It doesn't.

The core of Getchell's script is Grady's relationship with his loved ones, especially Carol and his estranged nine-year-old son Toby. When Grady uses the invention to reconnect emotionally with Carol, he stops valuing work over his personal life. The promise of this type of transformation was present in all the previous drafts of *The George Dunlap Tape*, but Getchell places it center-stage and devotes multiple scenes to the evolving relationship between Grady and Carol, while eliminating Rubin and Messina's competing subplots. In short, *The Light Fantastic* is a ruthlessly simplified version of the story, offering no hint of a cultural crisis or a cultural awakening, no concern about the revolutionary possibilities of Grady's mind-reading invention, no high-stakes conflict over possession of the machine. It's a relationship drama, pure and simple.

In the final act, Grady, Carol and Toby easily destroy the three prototypes of Grady's invention and thwart the bumbling bad guys. Then, Getchell delivers an ending that is light years away from Rubin and Messina's visions. Trumbull's three-stage grand finale appears intact (as the recorded experience on Midge's death tape), but the spectacular journey into death and the afterlife is followed—and arguably undercut—by a new coda in which a minor character finds Grady's house abandoned but full of balloons. The implication is that Grady has surrendered his work and skipped off to Tahiti with Carol and Toby, to enjoy more important things in life. On paper, this is a thought-provoking grace note—a simple expression of a simpler notion of enlightenment. On a larger-than-usual movie screen, however, such an ending would have been decidedly unspectacular.

Brainstorm (February 1981 Draft)

In the end, Getchell's script disappeared just like Grady Martin. (Today, it exists only in Special Collections at the Houghton Library at Harvard University.) In August 1980, MGM procured all the various *Dunlap* drafts from Paramount, and delivered a 117-page 'temporary complete script'—entitled *Brainstorm*—to the Margaret Herrick Library in Beverly Hills. This new script was attributed to four writers: Robert Getchell, Philip Messina, Bruce Rubin and Douglas Trumbull. Messina describes it as 'my version' augmented by 'a few of Getchell's character goodies'.[43] The draft also includes Trumbull's three-stage finale and a completely new lab rat character named T.J. Wilkins, apparently added for comic relief.

In the fall of 1980, the studio and the director were finally ready to move forward. Around the same time, Trumbull established his independent company EEG (Entertainment Effects Group) and began overseeing special effects work for Ridley Scott's film *Blade Runner*, with the understanding that he would pass the reins to a qualified colleague when his own film went into production.[44] According to screenwriter Robert Stitzel, however, the project remained in development hell because the filmmakers 'couldn't get a cast—they couldn't get anyone to commit to the movie'. Stitzel says it was for this reason that he was hired to do a rewrite in December 1980.

Robert Stitzel had been honing his skills as a screenwriter for much of the previous decade. After graduating from the University of Southern California's School of Cinema-Television, he worked as a reader for *Smokey and the Bandit* producer Robert Levy, and learned from the examples of the more than 1,000 scripts that crossed his desk. He became a professional screenwriter in 1976, writing the teleplay for NBC's Saturday morning horse opera *Thunder* (1977) and the NBC Movie-of-the-Week *Better Late Than Never* (1979). After that, he says, 'I had written a screenplay for MGM which they liked. It was called *Night-Blooming Jasmine*, and it was my take on *Chinatown*—a blistery, seductive movie. The head of production read it and liked it, and that's why they put me on *Brainstorm*.'

Stitzel admits that he was not particularly interested in science fiction. He describes his preferred genre as 'action with an undercurrent of emotion,' and explains, 'What

I enjoy is seeing people's reactions to conflict, seeing how people deal with being placed in awkward situations.' It was this emphasis on characterisation—the fact that *Night-Blooming Jasmine* had good characters'—that got him hired. He remembers, 'They had a script by Bruce Rubin, they had a script by Robert Getchell and they had a script by Philip Messina. I'm not sure if I even read the Rubin script. I might have glanced at the Getchell script, which was entirely different. It was kind of like a family drama. I don't remember what role [the invention] even played in it, but it was secondary to the family drama. No one wanted that script. So what I got was the Messina script, and in essence I did a page-one rewrite with characters, plot, everything. For me, it was an original screenplay based on Rubin's idea about this device.'

In a 1983 interview, Stitzel characterised his first draft of the script as a 'tune-up' of Messina's script, noting that he also incorporated Trumbull's ideas as the director conveyed them to him—although the ideas weren't always clear. He elaborated, 'I think Doug had a lot of notions, but sometimes they were locked up in his mind and it was difficult for him to communicate exactly what he was reaching for. A lot of what we discussed had to do with the basic tenor of the piece—if it was to be a thriller or a drama of enlightenment, or what.'[45] Today, he admits that he was 'kind of bored [with the story] until Lillian died'. The death tape was the hook he chose to hang his script on: 'What's after life? That was intriguing to me.'

In January 1981, Stitzel says, he was halfway through his rewrite when he was belatedly forced to audition for the job: 'John Foreman—who was the [executive] producer—called me in to read the script. I said, "John, it's not done yet. Let me finish." He said, "No, bring it in." Driving over, I was wondering, *Do I have a career or not?* It was a hairy moment.' When he arrived on the lot, he was ushered into an office with Foreman, MGM executive Willie Hunt, Hunt's assistant, and Trumbull. 'I think I had sixty pages or so, so I gave them the sixty pages and Foreman told me to sit while they read the script.' The minutes ticked by. Slowly. 'I'm sitting there while they're reading the script, and I'm trying to read their faces, [to see] whether they like it or not.' When the readers finally looked up, he knew all was well. 'At the end of it,' he says, 'if they could have put me on their shoulders and paraded me around the studio, they would have done so. They were very happy with what was going on. So I finished the script.'

Stitzel turned in his first full draft of *Brainstorm* on February 6, 1981. This draft opens with a giant movie screen displaying test patterns and a countdown to broadcast, then moves into the story proper, with Grady Martin, Lillian Reynolds, Hal Abramson, and T.J. Wilkins conducting experiments in the ICT lab. The basic plot is similar to the previous draft of *Brainstorm*, but Stitzel has made several significant changes to character dynamics and motivations. Throughout the script, he teases the notion of a love triangle between Grady, Grady's wife (now named Karen), and Lillian. In the beginning, Grady and Karen are polite but distant; both believe that their marriage is beyond saving. Their scenes together are poignant because they remain clearly vulnerable; both want to understand why the most important relationship in their lives has failed, but they simply cannot communicate effectively.

Grady's interactions with Lillian are equally moving, because she is secretly in love with him—and also because she knows she is dying. Instead of confiding in Grady, Lillian conceals her feelings and chain-smokes. Grady seems—or pretends to be—oblivious to the extent of her affection. At one point, he cluelessly asks her why he has so much trouble with women; the obvious answer is that he's young and naïve, but she spares his feelings. Because Lillian is older and wiser (and more cynical), the two opposites attract each other in a way that neither one of them will admit. For all three of the characters in this subtle love triangle, what is felt remains unspoken. This is why Grady's mind-melding invention becomes so important in their lives.

When Grady makes a recording of his wife's subconscious mind, he falls in love with her all over again. More than that: his experience of her thoughts and feelings redefines his understanding of 'self'. He says he's no longer a 'me,' but rather an 'us,' and tells Karen that he now knows with total certainty that people are more than their physical bodies. Stitzel says he arrived at the same conclusion in the 1970s, when he participated in a self-help seminar called *est*.

Founded in 1971 by social scientist Werner Erhard, *est* drew on a diversity of influences, including Zen philosopher Alan Watts and idealist philosopher Ludwig Wittgenstein, Scientology and Mind Dynamics, Dale Carnegie and Subud. Erhard's goal was to help students recognise and transcend unconscious patterns of behavior that limited their ability to live freely and happily. In an interview with his official biographer, Erhard described his personal awakening as follows: 'I realised that I was not my emotions or thoughts. I was not my ideas, my intellect, my perceptions, my beliefs. I was not what I did or accomplished or achieved. Or hadn't achieved. I was not what I had done right—or what I had done wrong. I was not what I had been labeled—by myself or others. All these identifications cut me off from experience, from living. I was none of these. I was simply the space, the creator, the source of all that stuff.'[46]

Stitzel remembers his own transformative experience in similar terms: 'I had gone through the *est* training, which really gets your ego out of the way. You're really giving up your sense of self, 'I'm right and you're wrong,' justifications, all that stuff. That's what I was putting into *Brainstorm*, that idea that you are more than you think you are. [The invention] breaks through all of our made-up constructions about how we feel about something—because it's all made up. We make choices based on events, and [the memory of those choices] begins to govern our life, event after event. I try not to live in my thoughts too much, and to live in the moment instead. What I'm seeing, what I'm smelling, what I'm saying.'

In Stitzel's first draft of *Brainstorm*, Grady's understanding of reality continues to grow as the story progresses. Lillian's death tape gives him a preview of his own death, followed by a horrific vision of an afterlife that the screenwriter—while restoring elements that Trumbull had previously discarded—likens to 'Dante's Inferno'. It also reveals a brief glimpse of the human world as it will exist after his death: a dystopian future in which people are hopelessly addicted to his invention. Upon seeing that, Grady resolves to destroy his invention, and schemes with Karen to upload his memories to her mind, so that he can continue to exist in some form for their son.

In the final act, Grady dodges the death he has foreseen and subverts the dystopian future, but at that point fate catches up with him. A government agent finds him in a phone booth on a rural highway, and fatally shoots him. On the other end of the phone line, Karen stands in an airport terminal with their son, preparing to fly away to safety. Karen takes off the helmet that has allowed her to view her husband's fate—but, because their minds are linked on a metaphysical plane, she continues to share his experience of life after death: the light, the tunnel of energy, and a series of miraculous visions. This time, instead of seeing 'Dante's Inferno,' Grady—and Karen, by extension—experiences an ecstatic vision of heaven. The script ends with a brief verbal exchange between Karen and her son. The mother promises him a future without fear.

In spite of this positive note, Stitzel remembers that the producers 'did not want [Grady] to die,' and made it clear the script would have to be revised. After Stitzel turned in his first draft in February 1981, however, a Writer's Guild union strike sidelined him until June. In the meantime, the script made its way to talent agents and managers throughout Hollywood. Stitzel had met his obligation, and soon major cast members began to sign on. Around that same time, Doug Trumbull handed off the reins on *Blade Runner* so he could concentrate on *Brainstorm*. After five long years in development hell, the project was finally going online.

Footnotes

20. Jung 241-242
21. Herzog
22. Farber: 'Brainstorming' 79
23. Seven, Crawley: *'Brainstorm'* 24
24. Guckian
25. Chase 67-68
26. Chase 68
27. Delson
28. Crawley: 'Wizard' 40
29. Morton 124
30. Anonymous: '1977'
31. Muir
32. Sobchack 226
33. Brosnan 262
34. Kael
35. Klemesrud
36. Morton 249
37. Munson 27
38. Moody 31
39. Guckian

40. Chase 69
41. Farber: 'Brainstorming' 80
42. Belton 39
43. Wolter 18
44. Sammon 225
45. Wolter 18
46. Bartley 167-168

IV. PRODUCING

Casting and Rehearsals

By July 1981, a stellar cast had been assembled to make *Brainstorm*. The lead role was assigned to Christopher Walken, a recent Academy Award winner for his performance in *The Deer Hunter* (1978). The role of his wife went to Natalie Wood, a beloved actress remembered for roles in *Miracle on 34th Street* (1947), *Rebel Without a Cause* (1955), *The Searchers* (1956), *West Side Story* (1961), and *Splendor in the Grass* (1961). Louise Fletcher, whose steely performance as Nurse Ratched in *One Flew Over the Cuckoo's Nest* (1975) earned her an Oscar, signed on to play Lillian Reynolds.

The cast assembled, from left to right: Christopher Walken, Joe Dorsey, Louise Fletcher, Cliff Robertson, and Natalie Wood in Brainstorm (MGM/UA, 1983)

The most surprising casting announcement was Cliff Robertson in the role of Alex Terson (a variation on the Robert Rankill character). Like his fellow cast members, Robertson had multiple awards under his belt, including an Oscar for his performance in the 1968 film *Charly*, but his involvement in a recent Hollywood scandal—detailed in David McClintick's 1982 book *Indecent Exposure*—had cast a dark cloud over his acting career. In 1977, Robertson testified in the criminal investigation of David Begelman, who was convicted of embezzlement the following year. After the scandal broke, Robertson had trouble getting work, and the actor concluded that he had been quietly blacklisted. He told *Starlog* interviewer Steve Swires in 1983, 'You could call it a coincidence, but from virtually the *instant* I exposed the 'Hollywoodgate' scandal, I didn't work out there.'[47] Begelman, meanwhile, made a lateral move from Columbia Pictures to MGM. No one would have guessed that Robertson would return to the screen in a film produced by Begelman, but that's what happened when he was cast in *Brainstorm*.

In the summer of 1981, director Douglas Trumbull staged the first official cast meeting at the Esalen Institute, a spiritual retreat center in Big Sur, California, where seminars were being conducted by transpersonal psychologist Stanislav Grof. Grof had spent years researching the psycho-therapeutic value of LSD, before turning his focus to the related study of near-death experiences. In his 1981 book *Beyond Death: The Gates of Consciousness*, Grof suggests that the experience of dying closely mirrors the experience of being born. He writes, 'Sequences of extreme emotional and physical suffering are followed by experiences of liberation, birth or rebirth, with visions of brilliant white light or golden light.'[48] Grof's seminars at Esalen aimed to recreate that spectrum of experience. Trumbull recalls, 'He would conduct these seminars where he had a slideshow showing the four phases of the perinatal experience: in the womb, pre-birth, birth trauma crisis, and release. In his seminar, he said, 'This is what movies are. This is what stories are. They are replaying this rite of passage. That's why movies have a beginning, middle and end. That's why movies have a happy ending.''

Trumbull, Stitzel, Louise Fletcher and Cliff Robertson all reportedly participated in one of Grof's 'rebirthing seminars'. Trumbull recalls it as 'an amazing experience' that 'bonded the cast and crew in an interesting way'. Louise Fletcher, by contrast, says, 'I couldn't wait to get out of it. We had one guy stand up and rip his clothes off and he was being reborn and he was a warrior. Doug was into it, because he had some idea about death. I mean, *please*. I'm too pragmatic and I just went along with it because I had to.'[49] According to Fletcher, Natalie Wood didn't feel the need to participate initially—but Grof and his wife Christina claimed years later that the actress was more open-minded on a subsequent trip to Esalen with her co-star Christopher Walken. The Grofs told Wood biographer Gavin Lambert that the actress took part in a session of deep-breathing exercises and meditation, and displayed 'grief, anger and finally a kind of transcendence'. They noted, however, that Walken was 'noncommittal'.[50]

The Grofs' work—and perhaps the cast's reaction to it—also seems to have influenced the screenwriter. An August 20 draft of the script introduces a number of superficial changes—George Dunlap / Grady Martin is now named Michael Brace, T.J. Wilkins is Gordy Forbes, Rankill / Rubinstein is Alex Terson, and ICT is EET (an apparent nod to Trumbull's company, E.E.G.)—but there are also some significant character changes and concept clarifications. The relationship between Michael and Karen is more openly hostile, the relationship between Karen and Lillian is more adversarial, and the relationship between Michael and Lillian a bit sadder. In one scene, Lillian suggests to Michael that they might run away and start a new life together; the moment is fleeting, and subtly conveys the pain of a romance that will never be consummated.

The most remarkable additions, however, are in new dialogue about the transformative effects of using the mind-meld machine. Michael pointedly suggests that his invention will stimulate a cultural paradigm shift—away from traditional Western philosophy, toward a more holistic view of life. In addition to echoing Bruce Rubin's original ideas, this dialogue seems to express the ideas of pop philosopher Fritjof Capra, who spent some time working with Stanislav Grof at Esalen in the early 1980s. In his 1982 book *The Turning Point: Science, Society and the Rising Culture*, Capra writes that the old Western paradigm is defined by 'belief in the scientific method as the only valid approach to knowledge; the view of the universe as a mechanical system composed of elementary building blocks; the view of life in society as a competitive struggle for existence; and the belief in unlimited material progress to be achieved through economic and technological growth.' He argues that 'all these ideas and values have been found severely limited and in need of radical revision'.[51] The brains behind *Brainstorm* would concur.

Another fleeting but thought-provoking passage in the August 20th pre-production draft is one in which Michael compares Lillian's death tape to a hologram, a three-dimensional photographic recording of a light field. Capra's book likewise embraces a hologram analogy, presenting physicist David Bohm's understanding the illusionary nature of reality as follows: 'If any part of a hologram is illuminated, the entire image will be reconstructed, although it will show less detail than the image obtained from the complete hologram. In Bohm's view the real world is structured according to these same general principals, with the whole enfolded in each of its parts.'[52] Unfortunately, this exciting idea did not make it into the finished film, which focuses instead on the question of life after death.

Stitzel says, 'The entire last half of the film takes off from the pivotal scene of Lillian Reynolds recording her own death on tape. Her memories and associations, and the images contained in the various tapes the characters play during the film, were carefully structured around the Grofs' research into the prenatal origin of adult neuroses.' Trumbull adds that, after his meeting with the Grofs, he knew *Brainstorm* had to conclude with the same kind of 'euphoric release' that the researchers associated with the final stage of the death-rebirth process.[53] Trumbull guided his team toward that destination.

In early September, less than one month before the scheduled start of principal photography, Trumbull convened the main cast on an MGM soundstage to read through the script. According to Stitzel, it was a very unconventional read-through: 'Trumbull sits down and he says to the actors, 'Let's pretend we don't have a script' and 'I want to hear your input.' Then it became a donnybrook, with everyone trying to be the heroes of the movie, and wanting their part enhanced.' Trumbull disputes this assessment, explaining, 'Every actor has strong feelings about how they can say something successfully, and how sometimes the written word on the page doesn't quite work for how they express themselves. I think that's pretty natural. And all the actors had something to contribute about how they would say some particular thing. It didn't change the nature or the content of the scene; it was just their personal way.'

To be fair, it seems that the screenwriter wasn't the only one who was nervous about allowing the actors to change the script. Trumbull remembers, 'I had a big run-in with [executive producer] John Foreman on *Brainstorm*. During the rehearsals, actually. We had moments when we would just go on an empty stage and do a table reading of the script, and one actor or another would say, 'Well, I can't say that. I can say what you mean, but I can't say it that way.' So I'd say, 'Fine, you say it your way.' And John Foreman came in and said, 'If you change one damn word on the script, I'm gonna call David Begelman and get you fired.' I prevailed and we continued to tweak the script and the dialogue all the time. That's a natural part of the creative process, and if you're working with your actors that way, they love that. They don't want to be forced into a creative mold. They want to have freedom to do some things creatively as well.'

In 1983, Louise Fletcher called the rehearsal period a 'rare luxury' in Hollywood, claiming that it 'helped enormously'. Cliff Robertson, however, presented the experience in a somewhat negative light, suggesting that the 'very democratic environment' reflected Trumbull's lack of confidence as a director. The actor added, '[Trumbull] recognised that he didn't have as much experience in dealing with actors as he did with technical matters, so he was wise enough to employ other people's expertise where he could.'[54] Stitzel has been even more critical, opining that Trumbull was in 'way, way over his head, particularly with this cast,' and claiming that leading man Christopher Walken seized the opportunity and immediately began 'wrestling power' away from the filmmaker.[55] The writer would become even more upset over the process that generated the final shooting script.

Brainstorm (September 1981 Drafts)

Just a few short weeks before filming was scheduled to begin, rehearsals prompted significant changes to the *Brainstorm* script. Stitzel remembers, 'We met for about a week, and Foreman had a stenographer there, taking notes for what everyone had to say. And of course I was taking notes too. At the end of the week, I think there was like two weeks to do a rewrite before they started shooting in North Carolina. I was given the package of notes—it was a compiled package and it ran probably about three or four hundred pages of our utterances about the script. And hell, it would have taken me two weeks just to read these notes. So I did the smart thing and didn't even look at them. I knew what I wanted to do with the script, which I did.

And I felt really good about it.'

The Turner / MGM Scripts collection at the Margaret Herrick Library in Beverly Hills contains multiple 'final' drafts of *Brainstorm*. A 'polish' dated September 11, 1981, further amplifies the Michael / Karen / Lillian love triangle, and adds Alex Terson to the amorous mix by hinting that his old 'alliance' with Lillian has been succeeded by his new alliance with Karen. Another addition is a scene in which Karen and Lillian connect for the first time. The scene takes place in a ladies' bathroom, where Karen sees Lillian take a nitroglycerin tablet in response to acute chest pain. Recognising Lillian's vulnerability for the first time, Karen realises that they have both walled up their emotions in order to build careers in a man's world. It is a rare moment in which the characters let their masks slip, and a subtle reminder of the buried lives that the film's invention is meant to unearth.

In a 1983 interview, Louise Fletcher offered context for such a scene: 'Lillian is a workaholic, and in movies that sort of stereotype is played by men. So is the part of the stereotypical driven scientist. There are women workaholics and dedicated scientists, though sadly not as many of them. Women aren't generally considered to be as self-destructive in that way.'[56] In this case, Lillian and Karen are exceptions to the stereotype—but for one brief moment, they relinquish their masks and recognise each other as kindred spirits. Stitzel recalls that it was Natalie Wood herself who suggested the scene. 'Karen was written more abrasive,' he says, 'and Natalie wanted to make her more sympathetic and more likeable.'

The new draft also attempted to highlight some of the loftier ideas in the story, with added snippets of dialogue about the ever-present nature of love—suggesting that it can be forgotten and ignored, but never truly lost—and the experience of being more than one's physical body. At one point, Michael likens the experience of sharing someone else's memories to an experience of 'Godliness'. This momentary use of traditional religious language might have been added as a setup for the script's simplified ending, focusing solely on Michael Brace's death trip.

The September 11th draft eliminates Brace's visions of the future, as well as Michael and Karen's mission to change the future by sharing his 'tape' with the world. Stitzel explains, 'There were enough fireworks going off, and that one just led to total confusion.' Trumbull adds, 'We hemmed and hawed around that for a long time, and it was really Christopher Walken and his very strong insistence that we were going too far—that we were trying to do too much in two hours' time—that made us change our minds.'[57] Instead of gathering material to subvert a specific dystopian future, the couple hacks into their company's computer system so that Michael can remotely view Lillian's death tape, and preemptively destroy his lab. His main mission is to view the message that Lillian left for him, controverting Alex Terson's efforts to bury the truth.

The script culminates with a sequence in which Michael plays out the final moments of Lillian's death tape inside a phone booth. Karen finds him there, slumped over, possibly dead. A cutaway shows Michael in a heavenly setting—not lost among the stars in outer space, but relaxing with his family in a backyard hammock. To Robert Stitzel, the scene was important because it grounded Trumbull's special effects ending in character drama. He reflects, 'What is heaven? It's love, family. It could have been a beautiful little moment—all this phantasmagorical stuff, and then this quiet, intimate moment.' In the end, Karen manages to coax Michael out of his heavenly dream and back to the land of the living, and the sun rises on their dark night of the soul.

A 135-page draft dated September 18, 1981, includes even more bits of character-defining dialogue—most notably, a few passages stipulating that Michael's new mission is to look beyond scientific data and knowledge, into the metaphysical secrets of the universe. The character is now desperate to know that his life's work has yielded meaningful results.

Robert Stitzel says that this version was his final draft of *Brainstorm*. According to the screenwriter, Trumbull asked him to submit his new pages to MGM's production office at the end of each day. Only later did he realise why. According to Stitzel, 'What he had done was to take pages that I was giving to the production people and rewrite them.' The screenwriter says that after he completed his work on Friday, September 18th, Trumbull turned up on Monday the 21st with a different script than the one he had submitted piecemeal.

Most of the changes made between the September 18th draft and the September 21st draft are dialogue changes, beginning with the opening lab sequence. The first scene featuring Michael and Karen Brace at home has been simplified, along with a subsequent dialogue scene in which they discuss their son and their life together. As a result, the relationship between the two characters is more ambiguous in the latter draft. The tension between Karen and Lillian, and the tentative romance between Michael and Lillian, has also been minimised. Lillian no longer snipes at Karen's design work, and there is no recognition of common ground between the two women.

Overall, the September 21st draft simplifies the emotional lives of the characters, and puts the emphasis on the physical and ideological conflict over Michael's invention. Some useful expositional dialogue about that conflict has been removed as well. In the September 18th draft, Lillian explains that she has intentionally obfuscated her notes, to protect her research from the military. She suggests to Michael that their work has a deeper purpose, which sets up a scene in which Michael realises that Lillian made the death tape in order to save him from her fate (death-by-workaholism). As a result, Michael becomes more assertive about his 'right' to view the tape and to see what Lillian wanted to show him. He confronts Alex directly, before scheming with Karen and Hal to remotely view the tape and destroy the lab. These details are absent from the September 21st draft.

In general, the September 21st draft would impose a greater burden on the actors and the filmmaker to convey the emotional lives of their characters through non-verbal nuances. The draft plays mostly to Doug Trumbull's strengths as a visual storyteller. The final week of pre-production generated a few more changes—including a rewrite of a dialogue scene in which Michael and Karen discuss the effects of viewing Lillian's death tape, and the elimination of Michael's 'heavenly' vision of domestic bliss. The final production script was updated to include these revisions.

Around the time *Brainstorm* went into production, Bruce Rubin offered this pithy perspective on the harsh reality of selling a spec script in Hollywood: 'It's a little like selling a house. Once you've sold it, you can't tell the people who bought it not to take the wallpaper off because you liked it. It's their house.'[58] Phil Messina offers a related insight based on his own experience: 'As soon as you bring a director in, the director's going to do whatever he wants because that's how the studios work. They let the director run. The desire to get a movie made overwhelms everything else. If you have a director who's not on the same page [with the writer], the movie becomes something else. That's the way it works.'

Trumbull reflects, 'I must take responsibility for not being very collaborative with the writers. I think they probably were pissed off about it, and probably have some negative feelings about it, which is okay. I was on my own personal mission, which has a lot to do with the actual medium of movies itself, and what you can do [with them], and how we can do something new and different, other than just telling a story.' To be fair, Trumbull was doing what directors are usually celebrated for doing—asserting a personal vision. When principal photography began on September 28, 1981, *Brainstorm* was unquestionably his movie.

Production and Tragedy

The Burroughs Wellcome Fund headquarters stands in for ICT in Brainstorm *(MGM/UA, 1983)*

Although Trumbull originally planned to shoot *Brainstorm* in the Boston area, he eventually opted for filming locations in and around North Carolina's Research

Triangle Park, a hub of science and tech-related facilities supported by three major universities (Duke University, North Carolina State University, and UNC Chapel Hill). The director explained, 'I feel it is important that real research of this nature is going on right here, in North Carolina, right now. We are here because North Carolina is beautiful... and we are here because this is what is going on.'[59] Among the locations selected for filming—and described in Stitzel's drafts—were the Burroughs Wellcome Fund headquarters (used as the exterior of ICT), a privately-owned 'solar house' in Chapel Hill (used as the interior and exterior of the Brace home), the North Carolina Executive Mansion in Raleigh, a hotel and country club in Southern Pines, Duke Coffee Shop, plus Duke University's Medical Center, Chapel and Gardens.

Trumbull made one final change to the script in order to accommodate an additional location. The final sequence in the film—where Michael Brace plays back Lillian's death tape over the phone—was originally supposed to take place in a phone booth along a desolate stretch of highway, but production designer John C. Vallone came up with a better idea. Vallone remembers, 'We had been discussing the ending and how it *had* to be special in some way. So, I said, 'Well, let's do it at Kitty Hawk.' It was sort of a joke, but it really turned out not to be a bad idea.'[60] Trumbull understood that setting the final scene in a phone booth near the Wright Brothers National Monument— where Wilbur and Orville Wright achieved the first sustained and controlled heavier-than-air powered flight—would heighten the ending's symbolic resonance. On that same site, Michael Brace would achieve his own breakthrough, soaring beyond death.

Brainstorm promised to be the biggest, most lavish film production ever based in the state of North Carolina. More than a month of filming was scheduled—but, by mid-October, *Brainstorm* was running behind schedule. According to first assistant director David McGiffert, who was hired to get the film back on track, 'a lot of the production was in chaos'. He observed that 'for some reason, it was difficult for Doug [Trumbull] to impart his brilliance, to communicate it to actors'.[61] There were other complications as well. Louise Fletcher says that 'the producers and the director didn't have a creative meeting of the minds', and Robert Stitzel blames many of the production's woes on Christopher Walken's 'aloof and indifferent' manner—and his influence on Natalie Wood.

Over the years, rumors of a romantic affair between *Brainstorm*'s leading man and leading lady have become the stuff of Hollywood legend. McGiffert told one of Wood's biographers, 'I remember someone in Natalie's hair and makeup group darkly saying, 'R.J. [Wood's husband Robert Wagner] is coming this weekend.' And then another time, Chris's wife showed up with very little forewarning, and I think there was a lot of kind of dodging and weaving that was going on.'[62] In his 2008 autobiography *Pieces of My Heart*, Robert Wagner remembers a visit to the North Carolina filming location in mid-October. 'During those couple of days,' he writes, 'the little bell in my head went off. Chris Walken was a very exciting actor and a very exciting guy who delighted in taking risks. The bell wasn't exactly clanging, but I was aware that I didn't have [my wife's] full attention. She was more involved with the movie than she was with her family, and the thought occurred to me that Natalie was being emotionally unfaithful.'[63] In an interview with Gavin Lambert, quoted in Lambert's 2005 book *Natalie Wood: A Life*, Wagner was more direct: 'It crossed my mind that they were having an affair, but I wasn't sure and didn't say anything about it to Natalie.'[64]

On November 5, 1983, the company moved the production to the MGM studios in Culver City, Los Angeles, for four additional weeks of shooting. At that point, says McGiffert, the dialogue between the director and his two stars became increasingly 'contentious,' with Walken and Wood 'aligned to what they were doing with the script'.[65] In an on-set interview at the time, Natalie Wood painted a different picture: 'Thanks to the rehearsals, we're all very familiar with our characters and how they feel toward each other, so Doug has allowed us to improvise some of the particulars which has resulted in a lot of unexpected humour.'[66] Her comment suggests that what she and Walken were 'doing with the script' was trying to find the right emotional tone for the story.

Although Christopher Walken has rarely spoken about his performance in *Brainstorm*, he has offered insights into his creative process. In a 2012 interview for *The Guardian*, Walken said he has never tried to get 'in character,' but has instead played variations on his own personality. He explained, 'There are actors who can transform themselves, famously so, but I'm not one of them. There's a crucial difference between an actor and a performer. I'm essentially a performer. That's where I came from. That's what I know. That's what I do.' In terms of preparing for a role, he said he rehearses like a dancer, 'looking for a rhythm' in the dialogue. Walken further confessed that he hates learning lines.[67]

Bruce Rubin, who visited the set of *Brainstorm* for one week in mid-November 1981, remembers, 'I was on the set and Chris Walken was not saying any of the lines. He was making stuff up. And I was thinking, '*But but but* those lines are essential to the movie.... How is this going to work?' I wanted Doug [Trumbull] to tell Chris, 'That's the wrong line.' Instead, he kept going. 'Okay, yeah, cut, okay, next'.' For his part, Trumbull insists that Walken's improvisations were simply the actor's way of keeping his performance fresh, and that he learned how to get the performance he needed: '[Walken] would take a scene that we had already rehearsed and perform it completely off the wall, and be shouting or screaming or gesturing or whatever. And I'd say, 'Well, okay, that's interesting, but why don't we just calm down a little bit.' And we would always get his take on take three. He would be right in the center of his optimum range on take three, and then take four would go too extreme the other way.'

The production remained troubled. On November 23, the final day of shooting before the Thanksgiving holiday, *Brainstorm* was four days behind schedule with thirteen shoot days remaining. That day, Bruce Rubin flew back to his home in Indiana, feeling elated that the film he'd conceived nearly a decade ago was finally getting made, but worried about how it would turn out. A few days later, the production was shut down.

*

On the morning of November 29th, 1981, the body of Natalie Wood was found floating in the water off of Santa Catalina Island. According to the initial news reports, she had been spending the holiday weekend there, on a 55-foot yacht owned by her and her husband. Robert Wagner reportedly noticed that his wife was not on the boat sometime after midnight the previous night, and reported her missing to local authorities. Shortly before 8am, searchers found her body floating in a nearby cove.[68]

There were only two other people on the boat that night: family friend and boat captain Dennis Davern, and Christopher Walken. Both gave private statements to police, but neither spoke to the press at the time. Initial news reports attributed Wood's death to accidental drowning—but the story soon took on an air of mystery. In a press conference on November 30th, Los Angeles Coroner Thomas T. Noguchi suggested that a 'psychological autopsy' should be conducted to determine how and why Natalie Wood ended up in the water in the middle of the night. Noguchi also claimed that police had information about a 'nonviolent argument' between Robert Wagner and Christopher Walken, which had taken place shortly before Wood went missing.[69] A few days later, the coroner's office issued a formal retraction of the statement, saying, 'We think 'argument' might be too strong a word. It might have been an animated conversation, heated conversation, a lot of conversation over a period of hours.'[70] On December 12, the investigation was officially closed.[71]

Several weeks later, Robert Wagner publicly shared his version of events, theorising that his wife had fallen into the water while trying to pull in a noisy dinghy. A close family friend related the husband's account of the fateful night: 'We reached the boat in a happy frame of mind after spending a few hours at the restaurant [on Santa Catalina Island] eating and drinking. During dinner, I got into a political debate with Walken and we continued it aboard the yacht. There was no fight, no anger. Just a lot of words thrown around like you hear in most political discussions such as 'you don't know what you are talking about!' Natalie sat there not saying much of anything and looking bored. She left us after about half an hour, and we sat there talking for almost another hour. Then I went to kiss her good night, and found her missing. It was only after I told [police] that she was dressed in a sleeping gown, heavy socks, and a parka that it dawned on me what had really occurred. Natalie obviously had trouble sleeping with that dinghy slamming up against the boat. It happened many, many times before, and I had always gone out and pulled the ropes tighter to keep the dinghy flush against the yacht. She probably skidded on one of the steps after untying the ropes. The steps are slick as ice because of the algae and seaweed that's always clinging to them. After slipping on the steps, she hit her head against the boat... I only hope she was unconscious when she hit the water.'[72]

In some circles, Wagner's explanation was accepted without hesitation. Years later, however, his account was publicly disputed by Dennis Davern. In 1985, the boat captain related a contradictory version of events, telling *Star* magazine that the 'argument' between Wagner and Walken was neither 'nonviolent,' nor about politics. He explained, 'Natalie lit some candles on the coffee table in the salon room and she and Chris sat together on a small couch, sort of a love seat. I was sitting across the table from them and R.J. [Wagner] was standing, glaring at them. Natalie was still flirting with Chris, hugging him and holding his arm. And Walken was doing nothing to discourage her. R.J. got redder and redder in the face and finally exploded. He picked up a bottle of wine and smashed it on the table in front of Walken. 'What are you trying to do, seduce my wife?' he shouted at Walken.'[73]

In Gavin Lambert's 2005 biography of Natalie Wood, Wagner admitted to smashing the wine bottle, and explained the circumstances: 'Walken kept encouraging Natalie to pursue her career as an actress, to follow her own desires and needs. He talked about his 'total pursuit of a career,' which was more important to him than his personal life, and said it was obvious I didn't share his point of view. It struck me as some kind of put-down, and I got really angry. I told him to stay out of it, then picked up a wine bottle, slammed it on the table, and smashed it to pieces.'[74] According to Wagner's account, that wasn't the end of the argument; Walken kept pushing, which prompted Natalie to leave the room. The argument continued until Walken decided to leave too. Soon after, Wagner says, he went to check on his wife and found her missing from her room.

Davern has become increasingly vocal over the years—and his account increasingly provocative. In 2009, he co-wrote a memoir entitled *Goodbye Natalie, Goodbye Splendour*, offering a detailed perspective on the Hollywood marriage, and outlining a chain of events that (according to him) culminated in an explosion of jealousy on the morning of November 28, 1981. Davern now claims that after Wood and Walken retired to separate rooms, 'R.J. was real edgy and then went below to go apologise to Natalie.' At that point, Davern says, he overheard 'a terrible fight,' followed by the sound of Natalie screaming.[75]

In November 2011, Davern's revised account prompted the Los Angeles County Sheriff's Department to reopen their investigation into the cause of Natalie Wood's death.[76] In 2012, a revised coroner's report drew attention to unexplained bruising on the victim's body, suggesting that the bruises 'could have occurred before she entered the water'. The coroner's office officially changed the cause of death to 'drowning and other undetermined factors,' and stipulated that the circumstances remain 'undetermined'.[77] The case remains open, pending further evidence—and the mystery continues to cast a shadow over the legacy of *Brainstorm*.

Death and Rebirth

After the tragic death of Natalie Wood, *Brainstorm* entered a limbo state. The production sound stages were closed and padlocked, to secure sets and materials until studio execs made a decision about if and how to proceed. On December 2, David Chasman, MGM's senior vice president of production, made this preliminary assessment: 'Natalie had five scenes left to shoot. Two of those scenes represented coverage on master scenes shot in North Carolina, and we could live without them. But two scenes were crucial. They set up the entire third act of the movie. They took place in a hotel room between Natalie and Chris, who were devising a plan to outwit the bad guys.' Remembering the 1937 film *Saratoga*, completed after the death of its star Jean Harlow, Chasman added, 'There is no question of the Jean Harlow solution—playing the unfinished scenes with a double in a big hat. Somebody will have to come up with a spectacular solution if we are to continue the movie.'[78]

Douglas Trumbull's assessment of the situation was very different. In a 1983 interview, he remembered, 'If she had died just one day earlier in the shooting schedule I wouldn't have been able to finish my film. The last day I worked with her we shot a crucial scene—the one in the laboratory where her husband records her thoughts about him on tape—thoughts that are very hostile. He then replays that tape and learns what went wrong with their marriage and is able to patch things up. Without that scene, I wouldn't have had a movie.'[79] With that scene in the can, however, Trumbull insisted that he could deliver a completed film with total integrity—if he was given the opportunity.

The director later admitted that Wood's death had necessitated a re-think of two significant scenes involving her character: 'One of them I was simply able to omit.

And, in fact, I now feel I probably would have cut it anyway, as I've cut out scenes which Natalie Wood did shoot.' The omitted scene seems to be the material that Chasman had declared 'crucial'—an intimate hotel scene in which Michael and Karen declare their love for each other, before putting their dangerous plan in action. Trumbull continues: 'The other was a scene that Natalie was not originally going to be in. Before Natalie was cast, the script did not include the female lead in this scene, but rather, another character. I simply changed it back to its original form.'[80] Here, he is referencing the scene in which Michael plays back Lillian's death tape for the first time; in the finished film, Hal Abramson (played by actor Joe Dorsey) would replace Karen as Michael's lab partner.

In the weeks following Wood's death, the debate over the proposed changes heated up. In January 1982, MGM chairman Frank E. Rosenfelt delivered the studio's verdict that 'the film was fatally flawed, that it was not reasonable and practical to finish'.[81] MGM lawyer (and future chairman) Frank Rothman later clarified, 'The position of MGM was never that *Brainstorm* could not be finished. I don't believe there is any picture that can't be finished, and *Brainstorm* was 90 percent in the can. But the studio made a creative decision that we could not film the script that had been originally approved. With the changes that Doug wanted to make, the film might have turned out less well than the original or equally well or better, but it was certainly going to be different, and that was why we felt it was not 'reasonable and practicable' to continue.'[82]

The studio's insurer, Lloyds of London, disputed the conclusion, and eventually decided to finance the remaining three weeks of principal photography—at a cost of roughly $2.5 million—so that Trumbull could produce a work print of the film for the studio to review and assess.[83] One of the underwriters described this as a 'salvage' operation: 'Think of the salvage that underwriters get when they pay for a hull loss and are stuck with a damaged ship. That is what we are doing.'[84] Trumbull reportedly worked for free, and convinced the cast members to return without contracts. 'Everyone was wonderful about it,' he said later. 'Nearly all of the crew returned and many of them turned down other jobs to remain available.'[85] On February 8, 1982, when production resumed, the stalwarts wore t-shirts declaring *Brainstorm* 'a Lloyds of London film'. It remained to be seen whether *Brainstorm* was in fact a 'damaged ship'.

According to Louise Fletcher, the final days of filming were 'very strange and very subdued'.[86] Cliff Robertson reported that the topic of Natalie Wood's death was 'studiously avoided'.[87] Everyone had a job to do, and they did it.

Eighteen days later, shooting wrapped—but the filmmakers still had a long way to go. In mid-April, a new conflict arose, related to twenty-five second unit scenes that had not been completed. MGM execs insisted that the scenes were supposed to be shot on the insurer's dime, and they refused to look at the work print until the scenes had been completed. Trumbull asserted that 'we were only to shoot those scenes necessary in order to release the actors and release the set'. He insisted that he had been explicitly prohibited from 'spending a penny on anything that had to do with second unit photography or photography that didn't involve principals'.[88] In early May, a court battle between MGM and Lloyds of London seemed imminent.

The standoff came to an unlikely conclusion when the director gambled on a risky maneuver. Trumbull decided to screen the work print for MGM's competitors at Paramount, Warner Brothers, Columbia and Universal.[89] When the word got around to the executives at MGM, that news apparently broke the log jam. According to Trumbull, the studio 'saw the possibility that another studio could pick up the movie and have success with it. Suddenly, they wanted to go ahead.'[90]

The director screened the work print for MGM, and subsequently began making arrangements for post-production work. In November 1982, he estimated that he would need an additional five months to complete the special effects for the film. Lloyds of London eventually agreed to contribute another $3.5 million in finishing funds.[91] Once again, *Brainstorm* had been resurrected. Ten years after Bruce Rubin wrote his initial draft of *The George Dunlap Tape*, the film was finally completed.

Private screenings were held for exhibitors as early as March 1983, at which time MGM solidified plans to release the film in two different formats. A 70-millimeter version would premiere in approximately 150 theaters across North America on October 7th, followed by a wider release of 35-millimeter prints on November 11th.[92] Preview audiences reportedly raved about the film at advance screenings in the spring and summer, which gave the studio confidence to launch *Brainstorm* a week earlier than planned (although Hollywood columnist Marilyn Beck suggested that MGM execs also wanted to avoid an opening weekend faceoff with the new James Bond movie, *Never Say Never Again*).[93] Following a hastily-rearranged West Coast premiere at the Cinerama Dome in Hollywood, the 70-millimeter version of *Brainstorm* blew into darkened theaters on September 30, 1983.

Footnotes

47. Swires 60
48. Grof 26
49. Finstad 334
50. Lambert 300
51. Capra 31
52. Capra 97
53. Wolter 19
54. Swires 60
55. Finstad 334-335
56. Scott
57. Munson 28
58. Fisher
59. Noblitt
60. Hutchison: 'Among' 43
61. Finstad 337
62. Finstad 391
63. Wagner 250
64. Lambert 297
65. Finstad 341
66. Chase 72
67. O'Hagan
68. Thackery, Anonymous: 'Natalie'
69. Noguchi 29-30
70. Maychick 126
71. Lambert 315
72. Maychick 132-133
73. Maychick 127
74. Lambert 310-311
75. Rulli 124, 163, 244

76. Winton
77. Goffard
78. Harmetz: 'How'
79. Atlas 18
80. Chase 74
81. Harmetz: 'MGM'
82. Farber: 'How'
83. Harmetz: 'MGM'
84. Shapiro
85. Thomas
86. Scott
87. Harmetz: 'After'
88. Anonymous: '*Brainstorm* Generates'
89. Anonymous: 'Brainstorm'
90. Pollock
91. Ryan
92. Brioli
93. Beck

V. STREAMING

The Grid

The final cut of *Brainstorm* begins with an opening credits sequence featuring state-of-the-art (for 1983) computer graphics, and ethereal music by composer James Horner. In a 1984 interview, Horner told *Starburst* that Douglas Trumbull had approached him about scoring *Brainstorm* nearly a year before the film was shot. Horner turned down a competing offer to score the 1983 film *WarGames* because he saw *Brainstorm* as 'a much more interesting film which has much less chance of being successful, but has the potential of becoming a very great film, in a way'.[94] Horner began composing the score while *Brainstorm* was in post-production. At that time, Trumbull was focused on creating the film's effects-driven finale, so the musician had to write to a rough cut and imagine the spectacle to come. Horner remembered, 'I'd call Doug up and tell him I'd need timings—composers work to specific timings. And he said, 'I don't have them, I don't have the shots done yet.' So all the specific shots in the film, he'd explain to me over the phone.'[95]

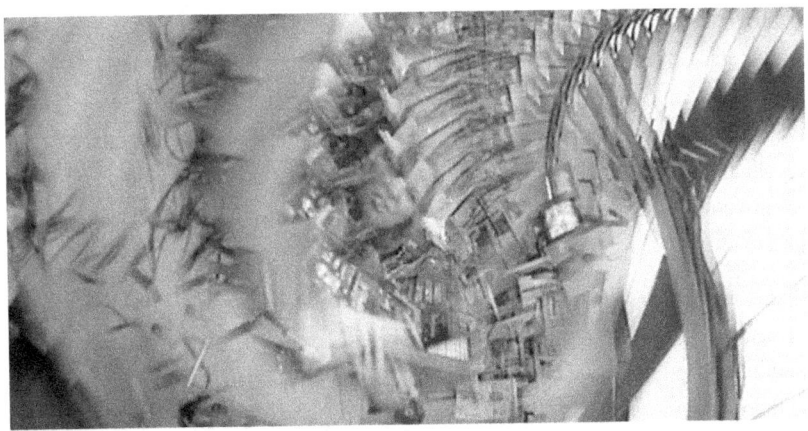

The vortex sequence, as featured in the theatrical trailer for Brainstorm *(MGM/UA, 1983)*

The first work-in-progress was the opening sequence. Trumbull originally planned to launch his story with a longer, more elaborate computer graphics sequence featuring a digital vortex. The effect was created and utilised in the theatrical trailer for the film, but the director ultimately decided that it would be too disorienting for audiences at the start of the film. 'I realised there was a good chance that the audiences weren't going to be with us at all if they didn't simply and concretely understand what the hell this machine could do,' Trumbull says, so he decided to start with a less confusing grid design, and quickly move on to the lab. The goal, according to the director, was to create a 'training scene' for viewers, 'to try and bring them up to speed with not only what the machine can do, but with the whole idea of experience as a way of learning something, rather than exposition telling you everything'.[96] The finished sequence gives the audience an intimate perspective on a battery of tests that demonstrate the invention's full range of sensory communication—including a comically disgusting taste test that combines steak, peanut butter, hot fudge, walnuts and marshmallow sauce.

With the same sequence, the director sought to quickly establish his characters as relatable human beings. Trumbull told interviewers that he wanted to avoid 'stereotypical' depiction of scientists as 'weird, difficult, obscure characters with no dimension or feelings'.[97] Accordingly, Lillian Reynolds and Gordy Forbes represent opposite ends of a behavioral spectrum. Lillian is intense, nervous, chain-smoking herself into an early grave; Gordy is boisterous, immature, and compulsively unprofessional. Caught between these two characters is Michael Brace, focused and unflappable. After a successful test of an invention that will almost certainly revolutionise human communication, he casually rides away from his lab on a recumbent bicycle, like an overgrown kid heading home from playing neighborhood baseball.

Upon seeing the finished film, co-screenwriter Philip Messina complained that this depiction weakened the main character: 'There is a prevailing attitude in Hollywood that a protagonist is someone everyone has to identify with in a literal sense. In other words, he has to talk like the guy next door, like one of Spielberg's Mr. Suburbia characters. I saw the character as being much more uptight and cerebral, less boyish than depicted in the film in the sense of riding bikes and playing with toys. The whole idea is that he evolves from an emotionally uptight guy to someone who sees all kinds of possibilities, not only intellectually, but emotionally. In essence, he becomes a man who gets involved.'[98] Messina's criticism implies that the film fails to create an emotional arc for the main character. In fairness to the filmmakers, however, Robert Stitzel's script(s) had already shifted some of the focus away from the hero's journey, and made *Brainstorm* an ensemble piece that didn't rely so heavily on the main character. Unfortunately, many of Stitzel's character embellishments are absent from the finished film.

In the subsequent scene, Michael arrives home to find his wife Karen giving a private piano concert for a group of friends—including a sneering fellow named 'Barry,' presumably Karen's new beau. The dialogue in this scene does little to clarify the state of Michael and Karen's marriage, but it's clear that something is amiss. The film then follows Karen to work, where she contemplates a streamlined design of her husband's invention for their mutual employer, Alex Terson. Two lines of apparently improvised dialogue acknowledge the friction between Michael and Karen, but don't bother to explain the cause. Their marital troubles remain uncommunicated in the subsequent scene, where they agree to sell their home.

By this point in the film, the viewer can sense a general reluctance on the part of the filmmaker to clearly communicate character dynamics through dialogue. It is not an unreasonable approach, for a film about a potential revolution in human communication. Screenwriter Robert Stitzel says, 'I remember a conversation with Trumbull, where I was trying to explain the subtext of the scene and he said, 'Why don't you just write it?' [And I said,] 'But if you write it, it will come off phony as hell.' Trumbull apparently took this response to heart. Significant chunks of dialogue were removed from the script between September 18th and September 21st, and even more scripted dialogue is missing from the finished film. The director was obviously less interested in developing conflicts between characters than in setting the stage for more direct kind of communication with the film's audience. In a 1983 interview, Trumbull admitted, 'I'm not very interested in script, drama and acting performances for their own sake. I'm interested in exploring what a film can do as a medium to create a super-reality.'[99]

The Hat

Brainstorm's super-reality comes into focus in a lengthy travelogue sequence that juxtaposes conventional cinematic storytelling (35mm film, mono sound) with a more immersive viewing experience (70mm film, six-track stereo sound). Michael, Lillian and their team make a series of virtual-reality POV tapes to insert viewers into adrenalising scenarios—stock car racing, bobsledding, hang-gliding, etc. According to cinematographer Richard Yuricich, these sequences were filmed using 'tremendous amounts of light and extremely sharp wide-angle lenses stopped to F5.6 and 8 to get a clarity of image, a depth of field, and a vibrancy of color—an overall *intensity*'.[100] When characters in the film put on Michael's invention, nicknamed 'the hat,' the unwieldy device beams the recordings directly into their brains. Audiences watching *Brainstorm* in 70mm experience the same thing the characters experience.

The virtual reality demos feature exotic backdrops like coastal Big Sur, San Francisco's Golden Gate bridge, the Grand Canyon and Niagara Falls—much like the Cinerama travelogues of yesteryear. In the 1950s, ad copy for Cinerama boasted, 'You won't be gazing at a movie screen—you'll find yourself swept right *into* the picture, surrounded with sight and sound.'[101] One ad went so far as to declare traditional storytelling expendable: 'Plot is replaced by audience envelopment—there is something that makes the excitement of going places and participating in adventure more than enough... the medium forces you to concentrate on something bigger than people, for it has a range of vision and sound that no other medium offers.'[102] Trumbull obviously hoped that *Brainstorm*'s heightened reality sequences would have the same effect.

The director's goal was to jolt audiences awake from their slumber of ordinary experience and expectations—not just during their time in the movie theater but after the movie ended as well. He hoped that *Brainstorm* would prompt viewers to question their everyday reality, explaining: 'Most of us experience life as a slow, evolutionary process, becoming so content with this pattern of reality that we seldom acknowledge that what we are aware of is no more than a small fragment of what we are experiencing. Yet every so often, something happens which is revolutionary, a dramatic breakthrough or event which is beyond our control and completely changes our perceptions of ourselves and of the world around us.'

Christopher Walken gives his 'memory mix-tape' to Natalie Wood in Brainstorm *(MGM/UA, 1983)*

In the film, ICT's board of investors is suitably impressed. One of the suits (Robert Jenkins) promptly reports his enthusiasm to a government goon (Jim Zimbach). Soon after, the military stakes its claim on 'the hat,' and a Machiavellian spy named Dr. Marks inserts himself into Michael and Lillian's research project. Once this central conflict is set in motion, character conflicts seem to disappear. Robert Stitzel points out that he incorporated dialogue in his shooting script to show that Alex Terson continued to fight—in vain—for the rights of his employees. In the film, however, Terson simply fades into the background as a greedy corporate figurehead with no sense of loyalty. Michael and Lillian's personal relationship is strangely nebulous, as are any plans they might have for the technology they've created. Lillian insists that she doesn't 'want to see it end up on some defense scrap heap before we know what it's really about,' but she doesn't speculate about what might be lost. The Michael / Karen love story slowly comes into focus, but Bruce Rubin's concept of the invention as an evolutionary machine is nowhere to be found.

Trumbull has said that, from his perspective, *Brainstorm* has two 'center points'. The first is the 'reconnection' between Michael and Karen; the second is Lillian's death.[103] Bruce Rubin concurs, noting that these two plot points appeared in his earliest versions of the story. A third subplot, also present in Rubin's original spec script, revolves around the character of Hal Abramson, who overdoses on a virtual reality sex tape. When Hal recovers, he tells Michael that his experience wasn't just a matter of psycho-sexual gratification, but some kind of upgrade. He declares, 'I'm more than I was, Mike. *More.*' This single line of dialogue reduces an important concept that was present in nearly all versions of the script, but it does at least imply a question that might be answered by watching Lillian's death tape.

Lillian's death is the second center point of the film, and actress Louise Fletcher went to great lengths to get it right. 'It took three days to shoot that,' Fletcher said in 1983. 'I did a lot of research for it. I had my doctor in Los Angeles introduce me to a patient who'd had a serious heart attack, and he described it for me in detail. I also got my brother, John, who works at the National Institutes of Health to introduce me to some doctors who'd had heart attacks. I told them it had to be a really bad one I experienced.'[104] In a 2018 interview, Fletcher added that Douglas Trumbull provided some inspiration as well: 'During my death scene he just sidled up to me and whispered in my ear: 'Eleanor Roosevelt.' I swear to god! I was 11 when Roosevelt died, and everybody on our block came out of their houses when the afternoon paper arrived and it said that she was dead, sobbing and crying and hugging each other, What are we gonna do? [...] He knew just what to say to me. What would mean something to me.'[105] The death scene is undeniably powerful, and what follows—an audio-visual recording of Lillian's metaphysical leap from everyday reality to the 'super-reality' of life after life—becomes the film's *raison d'être*.

The Tape

The second half of *Brainstorm* is essentially a special effects odyssey delayed and interrupted by moments of sober reflection and madcap levity. In the shooting script, Michael's experience of Lillian's recorded journey is preceded by a scene in which Michael and Karen contemplate whether or not he should play the tape. Karen expresses understandable concerns about losing her husband (again), which raises the emotional stakes of the film's grand finale. Michael ultimately convinces her that it's something he simply has to do, whatever the risk. His decision is comparable to that of Roy Neary (Richard Dreyfuss's character) in *Close Encounters of the Third Kind*, who essentially turns his back on his wife and children when he boards an alien spaceship at the end of the film. Unfortunately, Natalie Wood died before this scripted conversation could be shot, so there's little sense in the finished film that he has heard her concerns. In the film, Hal Abramson casually advises Michael to go ahead with his plan. Michael presses play and the spectacle begins.

At the beginning of the playback, Michael sees short clips of Lillian's life, building to a rooftop conversation with an unidentified man. The man asks Lillian if she's ever thought there could be more to life than work. She answers, 'I want to believe there is more, but I never could.' In the shooting script, Michael continues to play the tape and glimpses a tunnel of energy, followed by a nightmare landscape that the screenwriter compares to Dante's Inferno. In the film, however, the initial journey stops short, and Michael wakes up in a hospital bed, with Karen and Alex by his side. Alex strictly forbids him to play the remainder of the death tape, arguing that Michael's obsession with it is 'sick'. Robert Stitzel says he never believed in this characterisation of Alex Terson, maintaining that 'everyone would be interested in playing that tape'. Michael Brace, at least, feels the same way, and Terson's warning only strengthens his resolve.

A new scene, presumably improvised, justifies Michael's persistence—and establishes his wife as a co-conspirator. Sitting under the stars at night, Michael confesses to Karen, 'All my life I've had trouble with people. I didn't need them. Always had my own way, total confidence. Now because of this thing she left me—this tape—I'm scared. For the first time, I'm so scared. But the thing is, I like it. I want more. Look, you're married to the first man in the history of the world who has a chance to look at the scariest thing a person ever has to face. I've got to do it. I've got to play that tape, and you have to help.' Karen reluctantly agrees, but makes him promise not to ever leave her again. With that matter resolved, the couple turns their attention to the starry sky.

Soon after, Michael hacks into the ICT computer system to access Lillian's death tape again, and instead stumbles upon evidence that the military is weaponising his invention. When his son then inadvertently plays one of the weaponised tapes, he witnesses the effectiveness of their experiments firsthand. Philip Messina created the original template for this scene, in which the boy experiences a hyper-real encounter with primordial sea monsters in a drowning pool. Robert Stitzel later added a nightmarish snorkel that turned into a snake in the boy's mouth. According to Stitzel, however, the drowning pool scenario was scrapped after the death of Natalie Wood, for obvious reasons. In the film, Chris Brace suffers a nightmarish vision of his father, who punishes his curiosity about 'the hat' with the kind of aversion therapy that Alex (Malcolm McDowell's character) suffered in *A Clockwork Orange*. Dad barks, 'You want to see something? I'll show you something!' In the next scene, a doctor tells us Chris has suffered 'a psychotic break'. He then quickly reassures the parents—who have a death tape to watch, and therefore need to move on—that the boy will be fine in a few days. (Maybe the filmmakers should have gone with a 'panic attack' diagnosis instead?) Michael and Karen's hospitalised son is hastily dropped from the story, never to return. From this point forward, the plot of *Brainstorm* is a race to the finish, and the story itself pared to the bone, as Trumbull admitted in a 1982 interview.[106]

A scripted scene in which the couple verbally commits to a plan to destroy the ICT labs was not shot, and the subsequent sequence in which Michael's machinations actually destroy the lab plays out as slapstick comedy—with assembly line robots doing a Keystone Kops routine. This farce sets the stage for a much more portentous mission—the realisation of the film's 'ultimate experience'.

Trumbull's original idea was to take audiences through the most commonly-reported facets of a near-death experience, followed by multiple visions of Hell and multiple visions of Heaven. In the film, however, only one particular vision of Heaven gets much screen time; Hell is reduced to approximately ten seconds of un-contextualised closeups; and the NDE was apparently improvised. At some point during the final months of post-production work, the director decided not to try to replicate the accounts of near-death experience in books like Raymond Moody's *Life After Life*, and instead 'go into my idea about what death should be'.[107] The result was what he dubbed the 'memory bubble' sequence, in which hundreds—if not thousands— of individual motion picture videos appear alongside each other, creating a digital tapestry that represents Lillian's life-review. Trumbull described the tapestry as 'graphic representation of how memory might be stored in little slots of your brain'.[108] He further speculated that the memory bubbles could be 'part of some huge cosmic structure of nature,' perhaps an 'organisation pervading the entire universe that we all tap into in some way'.[109] His words echo Bruce Rubin's concept of reality as a living Akashic Record. Trumbull says he's content to leave the final interpretation to the audience, and he doesn't dwell on the details for very long. The memory bubbles quickly give way to a tableau of static images representing science and technology. These images slowly fall down the screen, leading us into Hell.

Douglas Trumbull's 'memory bubbles' in Brainstorm *(MGM/UA, 1983)*

Heaven and Hell

From the beginning, *Brainstorm* included a descent into Hell. Bruce Rubin's initial vision was inspired by a personal experience of death and rebirth. Rubin remembers his 1965 LSD trip as a Dantean journey into fear, culminating with the total annihilation of ego mind, followed by a slow, methodical rebuilding of perceived reality. Afterward, he concluded that what he'd experienced was a mystical awakening, and that his perceived journey through Hell was the necessary beginning of a lifelong search and deeper awakening. To put it more succinctly: He realised that had to go through Hell to get to Heaven.

Douglas Trumbull seems to have had a similar realisation during the 'rebirthing seminar' at the Esalen Institute in the summer of 1981. At the very least, he adopted Stanislav and Christina Grof's concept of death-and-rebirth as the basis for the Heaven and Hell segments of Lillian's death tape in *Brainstorm*. Trumbull says his goal was to 'construct a series of images that would create that sense of rebirth, hoping audiences would come away with some feeling that they, too, have accomplished something'.[110]

Whereas Robert Stitzel's shooting script references the art of Hieronymus Bosch and H.R. Giger in descriptive passages relating to Hell, the only vision of Hell in the finished film is a fleeting glimpse of pained human faces pushing through a membrane of bloody viscera—an image clearly indebted to the Grofs' teachings. In *Beyond Death*, the Grofs wrote about the 'terminal phases' of childbirth as an organic horror show, in which the nearly-born fetus experiences 'immediate contact with a variety of biological materials, such as blood, mucus, fetal liquid, urine and even feces'. Death, the authors write, involves the same sensations of 'wallowing in excrement, drowning in cesspools, crawling in rotting offal or tasting blood'.[111] The director describes his vision of Hell as 'sort of decayed and desiccated, a horrible place with thousands of people all meshed in it, caught, trapped, all sort of flowing down towards a big Devil's Garbage Disposal'.[112] (Perhaps an inversion of the *Close Encounters* 'Mothership ending', which was shot at Devil's Tower National Monument?) Remembering this Hell imagery from the finished film, Stitzel confirms, 'That was all part of the Stanislav Grof thing up in Esalen—that there's a rebirthing, and the rebirthing is like you're going through the birth canal, and [experiencing] the pain and trauma of that. That's what they were trying to create.'

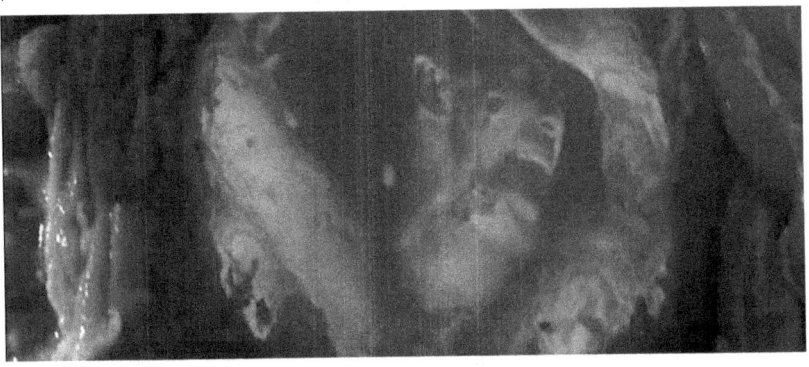

'The Devil's Garbage Disposal,' as featured in the theatrical trailer for Brainstorm (MGM/UA, 1983)

Trumbull explains how the horrifying images were created: 'Cow intestines were used in actual filming, the organs placed on a glass 'table' with an actor peering through from underneath, the camera supported overhead shooting directly down on the table.'[113] The resulting imagery is worthy of an early David Cronenberg horror movie—which is no doubt why it appears only briefly in the mainstream, PG-rated Brainstorm. According to Trumbull, when a rough cut of Brainstorm was screened for test audiences, audiences 'couldn't handle' this sequence.[114] As a result, the Hell sequence was trimmed down to approximately ten seconds in the theatrical release.

Interestingly, the nightmarish imagery was originally part of an elaborate plan for much longer Hell sequence. According to a 1984 article in Fantastic Films magazine, Trumbull also envisioned a set piece that his effects designers dubbed 'Condo Hell'. Actions Props and Miniatures Supervisor Mark Stetson remembers, 'It was sort of a basic Hades concept where we would cast up a lot of stuff and start assembling it in crazy perspectives, going off for no apparent reason—architecture gone mad, or industry gone mad, with a lot of meshing gears and threatening masks.'[115] Computer camera operator Don Baker adds, 'The Condo Hell image featured rows of weird, constantly changing faces inside vibrating helmets, slowly gliding toward the camera, set against an angular, architectural background.'[116] A short clip of this effect appeared in TV ads for *Brainstorm*, but no part of the sequence made it into the film.

Another unrealised vision of Hell was intended to depict the aftermath of a worldwide nuclear holocaust. This might have been a remnant of Rubin and Messina's original story, in which inventor George Dunlap sacrifices himself to prevent an apocalyptic future. The nuclear holocaust set piece was eventually replaced by Trumbull's more organic vision of Hell.

After the 'rebirth,' Trumbull planned a multi-tiered ascent to Heaven. Animator John Wash remembers an initial sequence that the effects crew dubbed 'Miami Beach': 'The idea was to rise up through the ocean, to break through the surface to go up to this fantastic city—then off into space. That would connect you with the space shots, with leaving earth. The city was supposed to be a humourous, fanciful kind of reality. We were going to create this city with an incredible layering of all these beautiful things and buildings surreally colored—like a super adult version of Disneyland.'[117] Trumbull remembers that his intention was to suggest 'passing through the present, leaving the material world behind—combined with a sort of birthday party, a celebration. Just taking a few seconds to look at the material world, treating it all very lightly.'[118] Ultimately, however, the filmmaker decided to avoid his 'city of light' imagery, for fear that it would undercut the grand finale.

With a bare-bones budget from Lloyds of London, and a limited amount of time to produce the special effects, Trumbull's E.E.G. team concentrated their resources on the climactic heavenly vision. The result is highly reminiscent of *2001: A Space Odyssey*, as well as *To the Moon and Beyond*. As in the beginning of *2001*'s 'Jupiter and Beyond the Infinite' sequence, the camera's point-of-view first rises above the earth into the dark vastness of outer space. Moments later, it confronts an expansive view of an entire galaxy—followed by many galaxies. Seconds later, this vision of a vast cosmos transforms into a miniature light show—created using bent wires, strobe lights, and streak photography. According to Trumbull, 'You fly through a whole galaxy from one end to the other in seven seconds, from the biggest to the smallest in the wink of an eye. Heaven, consciousness or whatever this awesome force is, might be inside an atomic particle.'

After this rush of super-concentrated images, the camera settles on a lingering view of 'Heaven,' an ethereal vortex populated by more than a hundred winged, luminescent humanoids. One possible inspiration for the imagery is Gustave Dore's 19th century illustrations of Dante Alighieri's visions of Paradise—especially the drawing entitled 'Celestial Rose,' which depicts a saintly throng of angels gathered in the shape of a multi-foliate rose. 'Celestial Rose' appeared as a full-page image in Stanislav and Christina Grof's 1981 book *Beyond Death*.

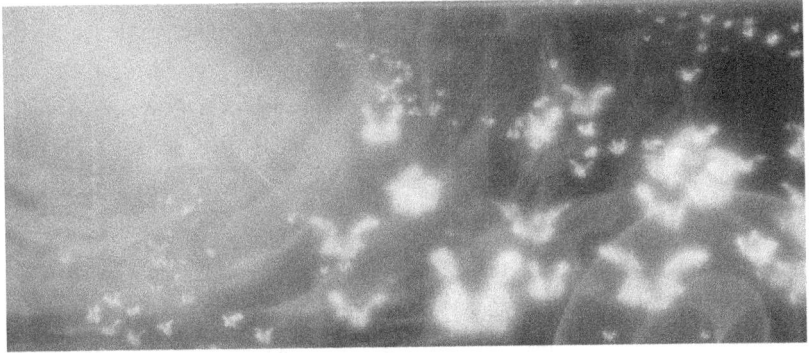

'The River of Souls' in Brainstorm (MGM/UA, 1983)

Trumbull himself has also identified John Milton's *Paradise Lost* as a source of inspiration, remembering depictions of a 'heaven like place where there were these rivers of souls—entities of some kind, not really angels, just organic shapes'.[119] He might be remembering artist John Martin's illustrations in a popular 1827 edition of Milton's work —especially 'Satan Viewing the Ascent to Heaven' and 'The Courts of God'. Whatever the case, translating this 'river of souls' to a new medium was no easy task. Don Baker explains that 'each angel had its own place and movement within the river' and 'the river itself would also move,' which meant 'a lot of overlapping motion'.[120] Trumbull adds, 'Each of those little entities you see floating along there is an *individual* exposure of a 35mm shot at 72 frames per second of a woman swathed in about 50 yards of China silk and backlit to create a weird sort of organic entity.'[121] Using a multiplane camera system, Trumbull and his team superimposed each of the individual exposures onto a single piece of film—about 100 exposures per piece—and optically combined seven different pieces of film with background imagery and lighting effects to create a moving stream of images with about 750 individual exposures per frame. The result is, at the very least, an awesome display of motion picture technology for 1983.

As for the 'organic entities' themselves, Trumbull insists that he never intended to create an explicitly Judeo-Christian vision of 'heaven'. Although he concedes that he and his crew referred to the organic entities as angels, he maintains that they might just as easily be called souls, entities, 'one component in the huge structure of consciousness or whatever you might want it to be'.[122] The director says that he himself does not believe in angels, and that he interprets the scene in broader terms: 'I see it as getting in touch with a more expanded consciousness or awareness of life, matter, the universe, energy itself.'[123] The purpose of the climactic sequence, then, is to prompt big questions about life and death and the nature of the universe, rather than to provide answers.

Brainstorm ends with Michael Brace returning to life, thoroughly giddy. He embraces his wife and points toward the stars. In a 1983 interview, Trumbull said he hoped viewers would have the same reaction: 'I'd like the audience at the end of the movie to look at the stars and stop worrying about their little world and think about this huge, awesome life out there. But at the same time, keep that in balance with your own personal life. The movie's really a love story.'[124]

Footnotes

94. Edwards 20
95. Edwards 20
96. Munson 36
97. Kart
98. Wolter 18-19
99. Pollock
100. Horsting
101. Belton 98
102. Belton 95
103. Hutchison: 'Douglas' 42
104. Mann
105. D'Agostino

106. Harmetz: 'After'
107. Hutchison: 'On Location'
108. Chase 72
109. Hutchinson: 'Douglas' 62
110. Kart
111. Grof 27-28
112. Munson 43
113. Horsting 23
114. Munson 44
115. Munson 39
116. Wolter 57
117. Muson 38
118. Munson 39
119. Munson 47
120. Counts 59
121. Hutchinson: 'Among' 37
122. Hutchinson: 'Among' 37
123. Wolter 19
124. Farber: 'Brainstorming' 81

VI. EVOLVING

Legacy

For nearly two decades after its release, *Brainstorm*'s legacy was that of a haunted film. The ghost of Natalie Wood remained ever-present, and the critical consensus on the film was damning. Most critics agreed that the film was a disappointing hodgepodge of ideas. Many of those same critics, however, were enthusiastic about specific aspects of the film, and a few were overwhelmed with enthusiasm. Ken McMillan of *The* (Chicago) *Star* newspaper gushed, '*Brainstorm* hit several points at which its emotional content (a love story, mixed with dangerous life-and-death conflict) and its intellectual content (the meaning of love, the search for scientific knowledge, and the question of life after death) merged with such force that I was, literally, swept with goosebumps, completely lost in the wonders and dangers that unfolded upon the screen.' In light of such unabashed praise from some quarters, critic Philip Wutch of the *Dallas Morning News* concluded, 'The plot doesn't bear up under scrutiny, but director-screenwriter Douglas Trumbull keeps things moving so briskly that only a grouch would complain.'

One obvious reason for all the 'grouching' is that reviewers had many different preconceptions about what kind of film they were going to see—or thought they had seen. Was *Brainstorm* primarily a special effects movie? Nearly everyone was dazzled by Douglas Trumbull's technical accomplishments. Was it a love story? Some critics praised it as such. Was it a revolutionary science fiction narrative, in the tradition of *2001: A Space Odyssey*? Or a gothic cautionary tale, one of Frankenstein or Jekyll and Hyde's many heirs? Perhaps because it had the potential to be so many different things for so many different viewers, it became all of these things for no one. In the early twenty-first century, however, some viewers have been able to look past the initial responses and appreciate *Brainstorm* as a pioneering work, a New Age hero's journey and 'the first Virtual Reality movie'.

Although released after Disney's *TRON* (1982) and MGM/UA's own *WarGames*, *Brainstorm* was conceived and produced before both of those tech-savvy films, and well before the term 'Virtual Reality' was coined. DVD releases in 2000 and 2009, followed by a Blu-Ray release in 2012, gained an audience of younger viewers who recognise the film's vision of the future as a present-day reality. Bruce Joel Rubin imagined 'a tape recorder which can play back the full sensatory range of the human brain'. Some younger Millennials might not know what a tape recorder is, but they can see similarities between *Brainstorm*'s invention and twenty-first century VR products like EPOC Emotiv, Oculus Rift and Google's Daydream VR. In 2018, *AV Film*'s Clayton Purdom observed, 'Many of the film's scenes can be mapped directly to the modern VR industry, including specific applications—porn, education, entertainment— and earnest discussions about form factor and user adoption.'

Other viewers regard *Brainstorm* as an innovative narrative that draws important connections between modern technology and the untapped potential of the human brain. Thomas B. Roberts, who in 1986 championed *Brainstorm* as an early example of science fiction narratives about 'the Hero as Consciousness Explorer,' points out that much has changed since the film was made. Filmmakers are no longer calling on 'quaint,' 'clunky' electronic technologies in such narratives, he observes, citing *The Matrix* (1999) and *Avatar* (2009) as 'transition films' in which psychedelic drugs are the technologies that 'prepare their heroes' for a transformative journey.[125] In his 2013 book *The Psychedelic Future of the Mind*, Roberts compares the human brain to a computer with an enormous variety of programs and applications; the apps, he suggests, are our states of consciousness. 'And just as we can write and install large numbers of electronic information-processing programs in our electronic devices,' he concludes, 'we can design and install a large number of bio-information processing programs in our bodies.'[126] Such programs could make us more intelligent and more creative—and perhaps that's only the beginning. This theory brings *Brainstorm*'s science fiction narrative back to the psychedelic experience that inspired it, for a generation of viewers that seems relatively open-minded to this cosmic journey.

Today, *Brainstorm* maintains a cult following that consists largely of viewers who recognise that the film has flaws but who believe that it is always worthwhile for science fiction cinema to reach for the stars—even if it gets lost in space along the way. *Mutant Reviewers*' Deneb T. Hall makes a compelling plea for 'pure science fiction' films in the post-*Star Wars* era, declaring: 'A true fan of science fiction should not forget that its original intention wasn't to dazzle people with special effects—it was to make them *think*. Stripped down to its core, it is the presentation of a scenario that takes scientific theories and concepts, and uses them to ask the most simple and yet most tantalising question the human mind has yet to conceive of: 'What if?' 'What if we could do *this*?' 'What if we did do *that*?' 'What if we went *here*?' 'What if we lived *there*?' Entire careers have been based on such simple queries. Most of them don't come with ready-made answers, just possible ones. The point is not necessarily the answers, if any, it's the questions.'

Bright Lights and Tech Noir in the 1980s

Bruce Joel Rubin, who won an Oscar for the movie *Ghost* (1990), is one such filmmaker who has built an entire career on simple questions. In 1981, while hard at work on the script for his mind-bending horror film *Jacob's Ladder* (1990), the screenwriter said, 'My purpose in writing films is to convey certain understandings about the possibilities of human consciousness. [...] Consciousness is usually limited to a sense of personal identity, but my objective is to indicate that consciousness can and does go beyond that.'[127]

What is consciousness? The story that Rubin conceived in 1973 to embody this simple philosophical enquiry, was part of the collective consciousness by the early 1980s. In the 1982 book *Who Dies?: An Investigation of Conscious Living and Conscious Dying*, American poet Stephen Levine unknowingly echoed the essential idea behind *Brainstorm*:

> Imagine if for the next twenty-four hours you had to wear a cap that amplified your thoughts so that everyone within a hundred yards of you could hear every thought that passed through your head. Imagine if the mind were broadcast so that all about you could overhear 'your' thoughts and fantasies, 'your' dreams and fears. How embarrassed or fearful would you be to go outside? How long would you let your fear of the mind continue to isolate you from the hearts of others? And though this experiment sounds like one which few might care to participate in, imagine how freeing it would be at last to have nothing to hide. And how miraculous it would be to see that all others' minds too were filled with the same

confusion and fantasies, the same insecurity and doubt. How long would it take the judgmental mind to begin to release its grasp, to see through the illusion of separateness, to recognize with some humour the craziness of all beings' minds, the craziness of mind itself? To be whole we must deny nothing.[128]

This is the philosophical conclusion of the Higher Consciousness movement that emerged in the late 1960s and abated in the late 1970s. Perhaps that short trajectory explains why, according to Robert Stitzel, there was some reluctance on the part of the filmmakers to play up 'the metaphysical aspects' of the *Brainstorm* story in 1981. 'Trumbull and I had a lot of discussions about that,' the screenwriter says, noting that he wanted the film to have an 'ethereal quality, [suggesting] that life is an illusion'. For some reason, he concludes, 'everyone got scared to do that'.

Upon seeing *Brainstorm* for the first time, Rubin and Stitzel both had a hard time separating the finished film from what they had hoped it would be. After repeat viewings, however, Stitzel concluded that 'it wasn't as bad as I thought it was,' and Rubin 'fell in love with it'. The originator of the screen story was especially taken with Louise Fletcher's performance, and the scene in which Christopher Walken and Natalie Wood exchange their memory mix-tapes. Still, Rubin says, 'I just wish they had carried the concepts to the fullest. No one in the world, except the few people who read the original script, know everything that was there.'[129]

Anyone who takes the time to consider 'everything that was there'—not only in Rubin's script, but in the revisions by Philip Messina, Robert Getchell, Robert Stitzel and Trumbull himself—must come to the conclusion that *Brainstorm* was a brain-buster waiting to happen. After such a strong buildup, disappointment might have been inevitable; big questions do have a tendency to overwhelm all answers.

Reflecting on the film's finale, Messina opines, 'The death experience by itself is pointless. That's the problem with the movie now. It's like an acid trip. 'Let's see what death is.' And who gives a shit?' Messina is not dismissing the philosophical question, but rather the main character's apparent motivation to answer the question. Why is Michael Brace so determined to watch Lillian's death tape? In the film, he gives a succinct reason to his employer: 'Nobody locks me out!' The implication: *Not even God*.

This answer might be construed as an unqualified celebration of the scientific pursuit of knowledge, but Messina doesn't see it that way; he argues that the finished film is mostly 'about self-indulgence'. The screenwriter believes that his script had more of a 'moral center,' because the main character selflessly sacrificed himself to protect the future. In contrast, the filmed ending has more in common with Steven Spielberg's *Close Encounters of the Third Kind*—not just in terms of spectacle, but in relation to the main character's willingness to abandon family and worldly responsibilities as part of his pursuit of (forbidden?) knowledge. Just as Spielberg's hero boards a space ship that will take him away from his family—perhaps forever—so Michael Brace casually risks losing his wife and son (who has supposedly suffered a 'psychotic break'!) in order to view the 'undiscovered country' beyond death.

In recent years, Spielberg has said that if he'd made *Close Encounters* later in life, after he became a father, he would not have ended his film that way. 'That was just the privilege of youth,' the director explained in 1997.[130] The ending of his 1982 film *E.T.: The Extra-Terrestrial*, in which a fatherless family saves an alien creature from faceless representatives of the military-industrial complex, illustrates his change of perspective. Messina likewise believes that *Brainstorm* would have been a better fit for the 1980s—a decade defined by rhetoric about a return to 'traditional' values after the excesses of the 'Me Decade'—if it had focused on the scientist's moral response to the nefarious appropriation and manipulation of new technology. That vision of the future might not have made it onto the silver screen in *Brainstorm*, but it did elsewhere—and with tremendous success.

In her book *Screening Space: The American Science Fiction Film*, historian Vivian Sobchack writes that the negative depiction of a nexus of technological and corporate power became a staple in science fiction films between 1968 and 1977. She points to Norman Jewison's *Rollerball* (1975), a film about a future society in which corporations have replaced countries, as a prime example. The trend continued well beyond 1977, as illustrated by the influence of monolithic corporate entities in films like *Alien* (1979), *Outland* (1981) and *Blade Runner*. By the time *Brainstorm* came around, some critics were complaining that the vilification of business leaders and bureaucrats had become a lazy habit for filmmakers. And yet—such dystopian visions were still far from 'old hat'. 1984 was just around the corner.

In that year, James Cameron explored the theme in his groundbreaking sci-fi film *The Terminator*, and returned to it again in *Aliens* (1986), *The Abyss* (1989), and *Terminator 2: Judgment Day* (1992). Messina reflects, 'Those are dark films. Post-apocalyptic. They're offering some hope, but they're also saying it could go the other way. The success of those films might have affected the [studio] response to the *Brainstorm* that Bruce and I wrote—but we were a few years too early.' Above all, the screenwriter laments the loss of his story's tragic ending, which he compares to Cameron's 1997 film *Titanic*, explaining, 'It's a love story about sacrifice. People die for love. [In 1983,] People hadn't seen anything like that since *West Side Story* (1961). People didn't die for love anymore in movies. To his credit, James Cameron understood that. He understood the power of tragedy.' One thing is certain: Cameron changed the face of science fiction cinema just as surely as Steven Spielberg and George Lucas had less than a decade earlier.

Cameron's apocalyptic vision of the future, which he dubbed 'tech noir,' was a far cry from what the director once called the 'candycoated' visions of those two predecessors. At the same time, *The Terminator* was distinguishable from the apocalyptic sci-fi films of the early 1970s by the storyteller's abiding faith in humanity. Like Spielberg, Cameron is a family man and a guarded optimist. 'I think of myself as an optimistic paranoid,' he says. 'And I mean that very, very, very literally. I'm very optimistic about the human animal and our potential, and I'm paranoid about some of the darker potential inherent in these technologies.'[131] One can only wonder what a filmmaker like this might have done with a project like *Brainstorm*.

Virtual and Expanded Reality in the 1990s

In 1983, Douglas Trumbull summed up his personal vision for *Brainstorm* as follows: 'We live in a society that's engulfed by high technology which we tend to take for granted, even though we don't generally understand where it comes from or how it works. So one of the things I was trying to do in *Brainstorm* was to make the audience feel comfortable with some of this new technology and help them understand better. But I was also trying to make it a little magical, to take the sky we think we know and sprinkle some more stars up there.'[132] This statement does not acknowledge or account for the thematic inconsistencies in the film, but perhaps that shouldn't come as a surprise. Trumbull, after all, didn't set out to tell a story in the traditional way. What he wanted to do was create an experience, 'a super-reality'. He wanted to turn the cinema into a safe technological equivalent of Bruce Rubin's experience on LSD, offering viewers the ultimate trip.

By the time his film arrived in theaters, Trumbull had come to regard Michael Brace's struggle as an analogue to his own struggle in Hollywood. In a promotional interview, he told interviewer Stephen Farber, 'In a funny way the movie is about what happened during the making of the movie. Christopher Walken is determined to play that tape, even though they take it away from him. Well, they took it away from me, and I said, 'No, you can't do that. I'm going to find a way to prove it.' The movie came to be very important for me, because it's about not giving up.'[133] After *Brainstorm*, Trumbull left Hollywood and immediately refocused his efforts to create 'a totally new kind of medium'.[134]

In 1985, he made three short films to demonstrate the potential of his Showscan technology. The shorts—including 'an unpretentious, thrill-a-minute race movie involving dune buggies' and a magician's tale starring Christopher Lee—premiered in prototype Showscan theaters at four Showbiz Pizza parlors around the U.S.[135] In 1989, the filmmaker formed a new company to create simulator rides for theme parks, including a wildly popular *Back to the Future* ride for Universal Studios. 'That was the next step for me,' Trumbull reflects. 'A completely immersive cinematic experience where you are in the movie. You are thrust through the proscenium arch into the middle of the movie.' The ride remained a fixture at Universal Studios in Florida and Hollywood until 2007, and at Universal Studios Japan until 2016—but, says Trumbull, 'no one ever came back to me and said, 'Let's do it again' or 'Let's do it better'.'

In 1994, Trumbull merged his company with the IMAX Corporation. Soon after that, IMAX became the gold standard in theatrical exhibition for a new century of science fiction cinema. *Star Wars* prequels and sequels (beginning in 2002), *The Matrix* sequels (2003), James Cameron's *Avatar*, Christopher Nolan's *Inception* (2010), Alfonso Cuaron's *Gravity* (2013), Doug Liman's *Edge of Tomorrow* (2014), Denis Villeneuve's *Arrival* (2016), and Steven Spielberg's *Ready Player One* (2018) have all been released in IMAX, along with countless other blockbusters.

Bolstered by this success, Trumbull continues to push the envelope. His latest innovation is a screening process called MAGI-pod, which he describes as 'a certain combination of high-resolution, high frame rate, wide field of view and high brightness in 3D that makes the scale of the screen completely irrelevant'. This time, the innovator says, he's not trying to replace the classic proscenium-arch drama—just make it bigger, brighter and clearer, so that viewers 'get to a certain point where the surface of the screen virtually disappears' and then can 'start directly grokking the fullness, so to speak,' of the experience. Trumbull is currently working on a screenplay for a film to convey the magic of MAGI-pod, which he describes as a 'current version' of some aspects of the *Brainstorm* concept, mixed with details about 'what I'm doing now'. It seems as if there is once again a significant overlap between the filmmaker's journey and screenwriter Bruce Rubin's story concept.

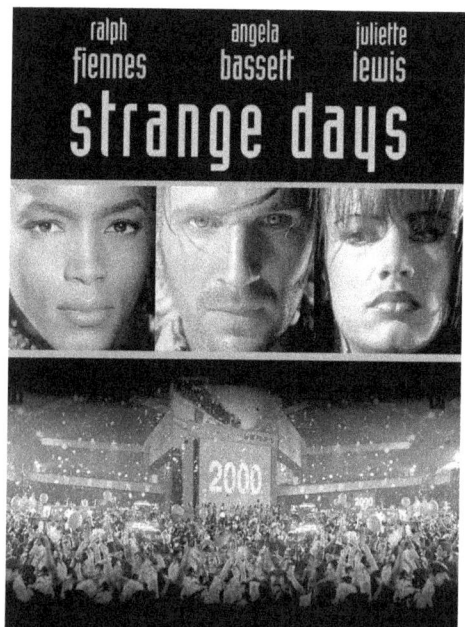

Brainstorm *was the primer and this is the advanced course.*

Fortuitously for Trumbull, audience expectations have changed a lot since 1983. Younger audiences, in particular, have a greater appreciation for the difference between passive entertainment and recreational entertainment. For some, traditional storytelling simply isn't enough; they need to experience the action on a more enhanced level. Since the early 1990s, *Brainstorm*'s promise of immersive reality has been realised through Virtual Reality technology. Hollywood storytellers began exploring this new terrain—at least, conceptually—in films like *The Lawnmower Man* (1992), *Wild Palms* (1993), *Arcade* (1993),

Brainscan (1994), *Hackers* (1995), and *Johnny Mnemonic* (1995). The VR subgenre came to its first peak in 1995, with the release of the James Cameron-scripted *Strange Days* (1995), about a black-market salesman who pitches *Brainstorm*-type technology like a drug: 'This is not 'like TV, only better.' This is life. It's a piece of somebody's life. It's pure and uncut, straight from the cerebral cortex. I mean, you're there, you're doing it, you're seeing it, you're hearing it, you're feeling it'. In a 1995 interview, Cameron summed up, '*Brainstorm* was the primer and this is the advanced course.'[136]

In the same interview, the filmmaker explained how he managed to focus the overload of ideas that had crashed the beta test: '*Brainstorm* had a lot of different, metaphysical elements in it, dealing with things like life after death. *Strange Days* is about memory, about the effect memory has on our day-to-day life.'[137] This description echoes the writings of William Gibson, whose 1984 novel *Neuromancer* pioneered the literary 'cyberpunk' movement. For Gibson, the main concept behind cyberpunk narratives is that human memories can be captured, stored, and transferred as hard data—and that our experiences can exist independent of the experiencer. If *Brainstorm* was the primer, then *Strange Days* was a cinematic distillation of ideas that had been a long time coming. On the cusp of the twenty-first century, as filmmakers and moviegoers became increasingly aware of Virtual Reality, the stage was set for a new golden age of science fiction cinema.

The Future is Now

Reflecting on the success of films like *The Matrix* and *Avatar*—as well as the growing popularity of Virtual Reality, Augmented Reality and Mixed Reality systems—Douglas Trumbull says, 'This is perfect evidence that people have always wanted movies or media to transport them beyond the everyday. They want something bigger, better, more immersive. There is huge interest in a spectacular, immersive, dramatic experience that combines the best of cinema, the best of drama, the best of storytelling, the best performances, and mixes it with something that just completely takes your head off—that disembodies your consciousness from your physicality and takes you... wherever. Into another dimension in time and space. Into contact with aliens or underwater worlds. Any of the things you can imagine but might not get to do in real life. There is a profoundly important human desire and appetite for that.'

Bruce Joel Rubin concurs. He suggests that the popularity of VR—and the renewed interest in *Brainstorm*—is symptomatic of a new cultural awakening, and he believes that the appeal of these things is rooted in a cosmic truth that spiritual teachers have been sharing for centuries: *Life is a dream, and we have to wake up*. The writer concludes, 'Life, as we usually live it, is more virtual reality than 'reality'. The Taoists call this a dream. Waking up from the dream is something that is going to be happening more and more frequently in the future, because the idea of virtual reality is such a familiar idea for people in the twenty-first century. We're going to look at everyday life and say, 'How is *this* different from virtual reality?' The truth is: *It's not*.'

Footnotes

125. Roberts: *Psychedelic* 176-177
126. Roberts: *Psychedelic* 125
127. Fischer
128. Levine 11
129. Dawson
130. Bouzereau
131. Greene
132. Kart
133. Farber: 'How'
134. Farber: 'Brainstorming' 82
135. Crawley: 'Big' 39
136. Greene
137. Greene

BIBLIOGRAPHY

Anonymous. '1977: Biggest Year in Film History.' *Variety*, Vol. 289, No. 10. January 11, 1978.

Anonymous. '*Brainstorm* Generates Headaches: MGM-UA, Lloyds and Trumbull.' *Variety*. April 28, 1982.

Anonymous. 'Brainstorm.' *The Sandusky Register*. June 17, 1982.

Anonymous. 'Natalie Wood forensic examination.' http://documents.latimes.com/natalie-wood-forensic-examination/ February 1, 2018.

Anderson, Ray and Shirley Meech. '*Silent Running*, or: Where Have All the Forests Gone?' *Cinefantastique*, Vol. 2 No. 2. Summer 1972.

Atlas, Jacob. '*Brainstorm*.' *Ampersand*. September / October 1983.

Ballard, J.G. *Extreme Metaphors: Collected Interviews*. New York: HarperCollins, 2012.

Bartley, W.W. III. *Werner Erhard: The Transformation of a Man, The Founding of* est. New York: Clarkson, 1978.

Bauer, Erik. 'Two Hours to Make a Deep Impact: An Interview with Bruce Joel Rubin.' *Creative Screenwriting*, Vol. 5, No. 4. July/August 1998.

Beck, Marilyn. 'Robert Wagner Upset About Film's Dedication.' *Chicago Tribune*. September 15, 1983.

Belton, John. *Widescreen Cinema*. Cambridge: Harvard UP, 1992.

Bouzereau, Laurent (director). 'The Making of *Close Encounters of the Third Kind*.' Columbia TriStar Home Entertainment, 2001. DVD.

Bozung, Justin. 'Douglas Trumbull on *Silent Running* (1972).' TVStoreOnline Blog. December 9, 2014. http://blog.tvstoreonline.com/2014/12/douglas-trumbull-on-silent-running-1971.html

Brioli, Susan. '*Brainstorm* on the Mind Again.' *Durham Morning Herald*. March 22, 1983.

Brosnan, John. *The Cinema of Science Fiction: Future Tense*. New York: St. Martin's, 1978.

Capra, Fritjof. *The Turning Point: Science, Society and the Rising Culture*. Toronto: Bantam, 1982.

Chase, Donald. '*Brainstorm*, At Last…' *Millimeter*. May 1983.

Ciment, Michel. 'The Odyssey of Stanley Kubrick: Part 3: Toward the Infinite—2001.' 1968. *Focus on The Science Fiction Film*. Ed. William Johnson. Upper Saddle River, NJ: Prentice-Hall, 1972.

Clarens, Carlos. *An Illustrated History of the Horror Film*. New York: Putnam, 1967.

Crawley, Tony. 'Big Screen Entertainment.' *Starburst* #84. August 1985.

Crawley, Tony. 'Douglas Trumbull: The Wizard of Special Effects.' *Starburst* #7. March 1979.

Crawley, Tony. 'Douglas Trumbull on *Brainstorm*.' *Starburst* #66. February 1984.

D'Agostino, Ryan and Eleanor Hildebrandt. 'The True Story of the Lost Sci-Fi Movie *Brainstorm*, Natalie Wood's Last Film.' PopularMechanics.com. December 21, 2018. https://www.popularmechanics.com/culture/movies/a25654064/sci-fi-movie-brainstorm-natalie-wood-final-film/

Dawson, Greg. 'Writer Rubin Ponders Puzzles of *Brainstorm*.' The (Bloomington) *Herald-Telephone*. November 1, 1983.

Delson, James. 'A Definitive Interview with the Outspoken Douglas Trumbull, Engineer/Wizard of Cinematic Special Effects.' *Fantastic Films* #3. August 1978.

Dick, Philip K. *The Exegesis of Philip K. Dick*. Ed. Pamela Jackson and Jonathan Lethem. New York: Houghton, 2011.

Edwards, Phil. 'Scoring *Brainstorm*.' *Starburst* #66. February 1984.

Farber, Stephen. 'Brainstorming.' *Film Comment*, Vol. 19, No. 5. September/October 1983.

Farber, Stephen. 'How the Battle to Bring *Brainstorm* to the Screen Was Won.' *The New York Times*. September 25, 1985.

Finstad, Suzanne. *Natasha: The Biography of Natalie Wood*. New York: Harmony, 2001.

Fisher, Jim. 'Hollywood Buys Screenplay from DeKalb Resident.' *The* (DeKalb) *Daily Chronicle*. August 9, 1981.

Goffard, Christopher, Kate Mather and Richard Winton. 'L.A. County Coroner Changes Natalie Wood's Cause of Death.' *Los Angeles Times*. January 14, 2013.

Greene, Ray. 'Rich and Strange.' 1995. *James Cameron: Interviews*. Ed. Brent Dunham. Jackson: University Press of Mississippi, 2012.

Grof, Stanislav and Christina Grof. *Beyond Death: The Gates of Consciousness*. London: Thames & Hudson, 1981.

Guckian, Brian. 'Douglas Trumbull—A Conversation. Douglas Trumbull, interviewed by Wolfram Hannemann, 10 May 2012.' In70mm.com. http://www.in70mm.com/news/2012/trumbull_interview/index.htm

Hall, Deneb T. 'Deneb Does Brainstorm.' *Mutant Reviewers*. December 11, 2012. https://mutantreviewers.wordpress.com/2012/12/11/deneb-does-brainstorm/

Harmetz, Aljean. 'After Tragedy, *Brainstorm* Resumes.' *The New York Times*. February 17, 1982.

Harmetz, Aljean. 'How MGM Protected $12 Million Natalie Wood Film.' *The New York Times*. December 2, 1981.

Harmetz, Aljean. 'MGM to Finish Natalie Wood Film.' *The New York Times*. January 27, 1982.

Herzog, Arthur. 'Science Fiction Movies Are Catching on in a Weary America.' *The New York Times*. August 25, 1974.

Hodgens, Richard. 'A Brief, Tragical History of the Science Fiction Film.' 1959. *Focus on The Science Fiction Film*. Ed. William Johnson. Upper Saddle River, NJ: Prentice-Hall, 1972.

Horsting, Jessie. 'Director Douglas Trumbull Envisions the Ultimate Experience.' *Fantastic Films* #37. January 1984.

Hutchison, David. 'Among the Minds of *Brainstorm*.' *Starlog* # 78. January 1984.

Hutchison, David. 'Douglas Trumbull: Between the Minds of *Brainstorm*.' *Starlog* # 77. December 1983.

Hutchison, David. 'On Location with Doug Trumbull and *Brainstorm*.' *Starlog* # 55. February 1982.

Jung, C.G. *The Essential Jung: Selected Writings*. Ed. Anthony Storr. Princeton UP, 1983.

Kael, Pauline. '*Close Encounters of the Third Kind*: The Greening of the Solar System.' *The New Yorker*. November 28, 1977.

Kart, Larry. 'There's More to the *Brainstorm* Story Than Natalie Wood Tragedy.' *Chicago Tribune*. October 2, 1983.

Kermode, Mark. *Silent Running*. Basingstoke: Palgrave, 2014.

Klemesrud, Judy. 'Can He Make the *Jaws* of Outer Space?' *The New York Times*. May 15, 1977.

Lambert, Gavin. *Natalie Wood: A Life*. New York: Back Stage, 2005.

Levine, Stephen. *Who Dies?: An Investigation of Conscious Living and Conscious Dying*. New York: Anchor, 1982.

Mann, Roderick. '*Brainstorm*: A Heady Role for Fletcher.' *Los Angeles Times*. September 13, 1983.

Maychick, Diana. *Heart to Heart with Robert Wagner*. New York: St. Martin's, 1986.

McLuhan, Marshall. *Understanding Media: The Extensions of Man*. Cambridge: MIT Press, 1994.

McMillan, Ken. '*Brainstorm* Satisfies Science Fiction Addicts and Wood's Mourners.' *The* (Chicago) *Star*. October 16, 1983.

Moody, Raymond A. Jr. *Reflections on Life After Life*. New York: Bantam, 1977.

Morton, Ray. *Close Encounters of the Third Kind: The Making of Steven Spielberg's Classic Film*. New York: Applause, 2007.

Muir, John Kenneth. *Science Fiction and Fantasy Films of the 1970s*. Scotts Valley, CA: CreateSpace, 2013.

Munson, Brad. '*Brainstorm*: Getting the Cookie at the End.' *Cinefex* #14. October 1983.

Noblitt. Bill. 'State Puts Best Foot Forward for the Movie *Brainstorm*.' *The Wilson Daily Times*. October 1, 1981.

Noguchi, Thomas T. and Joseph DiMona. *Coroner*. New York: Simon & Schuster, 1983.

O'Hagan, Sean. 'Christopher Walken: 'No matter who I play, it's me.' *The Guardian*. December 1, 2012.

Pollock, Dale. 'Trumbull's Tale of *Brainstorm* Trials.' *Los Angeles Times*. September 23, 1983.

Purdom, Clayton. '*Brainstorm* Turned Virtual Reality into the Orgasm Machine That Keeps on Giving.' AVClub.com. April 11, 2018.

Roberts, Thomas B. '*Brainstorm*: A Psychological Odyssey.' *Journal of Humanistic Psychology*. Vol. 26, No. 1. Winter 1986.

Roberts, Thomas B. *The Psychedelic Future of the Mind*. Rochester, VT: Park Street, 2013.

Rudi. *Spiritual Cannibalism*. Cambridge, Massachusetts: Rudra Press, 1987.

Ryan, Demond. 'A Director Who Never Gave Up on His Film.' *Philadelphia Inquirer*. October 12, 1983.

Sammon, Paul M. *Future Noir: The Making of Blade Runner*. New York: HarperPrism, 1996.

Scott, Vernon. 'Natalie Wood's Curtain Call.' *The* (Munessen) *Valley Independent*. September 29, 1983.

Seven, John. 'Interview: Douglas Trumbull.' July 7, 2009. https://medium.com/johndamnseven/douglas-trumbull-cf3f03171676

Shapiro, Stacy. 'Lloyd's Hopes *Brainstorm* Will Pay Off.' *Business Insurance*. October 10, 1983.

Sobchack, Vivian. *Screening Space: The American Science Fiction Film*. New Brunswick, NJ: Rutgers, 1987.

Swires, Steve. 'From Blacklist to *Brainstorm*—Sometimes Nice Guys Do Finish First.' *Starlog* #73. August 1983.

Thackery, Ted Jr. 'Natalie Wood Found Dead Off Catalina.' *Los Angeles Times*. November 30, 1981.

Thomas, Bob. 'Director's efforts pay off; Natalie's last film opening.' *The New American* (Santa Fe). September 23, 1983.

Wagner, Robert J. and Scott Eyman. *Pieces of My Heart: A Life*. New York: HarperCollins, 2008.

Winton, Richard, Sam Allen and Andrew Blankstein. 'Sheriff's Department Reopens Natalie Wood Case.' *Los Angeles Times*. November 18, 2011.

Wolter, Charlotte and Kyle Counts. '*Brainstorm*: When It Comes to Science Fiction Films, Douglas Trumbull Has a Better Idea.' *Cinefantastique*, Vol. 14, No. 2. December 1983 / January 1984.

Wutch, Philip. '*Brainstorm* a Visual Success.' *The Dallas Morning News*. October 6, 1983.

www.ingramcontent.com/pod-product-compliance
Lightning Source LLC
Chambersburg PA
CBHW071414300426
44114CB00016B/2302